PRAISE FOR *GOD UNBOUND*

Can you imagine a God who wants to bless all the families of the earth? A God who is greater than our anxious fears? A God who is known most completely in the tradition behind our tradition—in the risen Christ, who will never abandon us? In *God Unbound*, Elaine Heath contemplates the streams of scripture, ecclesiology, family systems, and spiritual practice in the call for a church that is at once mystical and missional. The result is a holy fire, a pearl of great price, an altar call. The church needs this word in the present moment.

—KEN CARTER
Resident Bishop, Florida Area
The United Methodist Church

Rare is the theologian who can be both clear-eyed about the mess the church is in and genuinely inspiring about what God can yet do. Elaine Heath does both beautifully. She is one of the most important voices we have in Methodism and indeed in the church universal. When new communities of Jesus' followers emerge from the ruins of Christendom, they'll have Heath's work in hand, lovingly dog-eared and underlined.

—JASON BYASSEE
Butler Chair in Homiletics and Biblical Hermeneutics
Vancouver School of Theology

Elaine Heath provides ancient wisdom for an anxious church. *God Unbound* will be enormously helpful to those innovating new forms of church and mission and to those in more traditional settings struggling to understand them.

—GRAHAM HORSLEY
Connexional Fresh Expressions Missioner
British Conference of the Methodist Church

GOD UNBOUND

WISDOM FROM GALATIANS FOR THE ANXIOUS CHURCH

ELAINE A. HEATH

UPPER
ROOM BOOKS®
NASHVILLE

Cover design: Bruce Gore, Gorestudio.inc
Cover illustration: Shutterstock Images

LIBRARY OF CONGRESS CATALOGING-IN-PUBLICATION DATA
Names: Heath, Elaine A., 1954– author.
Title: God unbound : wisdom from Galatians for the anxious church / Elaine A.
Heath.
Description: Nashville : Upper Room Books, 2016. | Includes bibliographical references.
Identifiers: LCCN 2016005204| ISBN 9780835815833 (print) | ISBN 9780835815840 (mobi) | ISBN 9780835815857 (epub)
Subjects: LCSH: Bible. Galatians—Criticism, interpretation, etc.
Classification: LCC BS2685.52 .H43 2016 | DDC 227/.406—dc23
LC record available at http://lccn.loc.gov/2016005204

For

Reverend Ceciliah Igweta and Reverend Jacob Keega,
my beloved friends and colleagues who daily help the church
live into Ubuntu wisdom:

I am because we are; we are because I am.

CONTENTS

An Unexpected Problem with Paul

I HAVE NEVER BEEN a traditionalist in the the way that most church people understand the word. I have spent the past three decades urging the church to get out of its buildings and into the world. The ancient Celtic monks serve as my heroes because they set out to sea in small boats with neither paddle nor sail, trusting the Wild Goose to guide them along.[1] Wherever they landed became their new home, a place where they created new, gospel-bearing, culturally relevant traditions. I have written about reclaiming the wisdom of the mystics, saints, and martyrs, in part, because they teach us to detach from our death grip on traditions that have taken the place of God.[2]

In my work I have exhorted the church to move away from staid traditionalism into dynamic, spiritually deep yet nimble expressions of church—the kind that twentieth-century spiritual giants Dietrich Bonhoeffer, Karl Rahner, Thomas Merton, and Henri Nouwen claimed will be necessary for the church to exist in the decades ahead.[3] Bonhoeffer referred to the church of the future as a new kind of monasticism that enfleshes the Sermon on the Mount.

With these prophets and others I believe we must now take up the gospel-shaped movement of Jesus. We must now live into a new kind of monasticism, one without walls or cloister, one that has little in common with the old monasticism as Bonhoeffer said, one that finds solidarity with "the least of these" and is accessible to and largely led by laypeople.

> **The gospel-shaped church is the only kind that will birth Jesus-followers in the years ahead.**

A broad grassroots movement is rising—global and God-breathed. It looks much more like original Methodism (in many ways a lay monastic movement) than what passes for church today. It is imperative that the institutional church that is collapsing beneath bureaucratic top heaviness, clergy-centric practice, and ecclesiastic loss of soul live forward into the original vision of Jesus. Indeed, the gospel-shaped church is the only kind that will birth Jesus-followers in the years ahead. What I see emerging in myriad ways and places is precisely that—a gospel-shaped movement.

This conviction drives more than my research, writing, and teaching. During the past several years my husband and I have chosen to live in intentional Christian community, taking up new monastic rhythms of prayer, hospitality, and justice. I have worked with friends and students to plant diverse experimental communities that serve as contextual laboratories for on-the-ground learning.[4] As more and more people developed an interest in our Missional Wisdom communities, we created training opportunities for them. Whether clergy or laity, increasing numbers of people within the church feel called to develop faith communities beyond the walls of the church. They serve as emerging leaders of what God is sprouting from the cracks in the crumbling foundation of church as we've known it.

The incubation, hatching, and flowering of many missional, new-monastic learning initiatives has filled the past decade.[5] These initiatives help the church move beyond its fearful, clutching, backward-looking stuckness, a malady that the anxious most often describe as "holding on to our tradition." What they fear losing most assuredly is not universal tradition, ancient tradition, or global tradition. What they call tradition refers primarily to the habitual in their own context—a tradition of sorts but with a small *t*.

A Shocking Discovery

I spend a lot of time thinking about these matters. So imagine my shock one day when I suddenly found myself on the side of Paul's detractors: the Traditionalists. I had begun reading Paul's epistle to the Galatians again as part of my morning prayer. I have read this epistle many times—in Greek and in numerous English translations. I have parsed it, taught it, preached from it, treasured it. Martin Luther described this book as his lover, his spouse, his Katharina von Bora. It is the book for reformers. It was the book for me.

Landing on the Wrong Side

This day, though, I found Paul annoying. Even more, I felt threatened by his freewheeling words. The idea that Gentiles could be just as close to the God of the Jews without Jewish tradition, that thousands of years of sacred history recalled through precise liturgical practice were unnecessary, that God wasn't particularly Jewish after all, did not seem like good news.[6] It seemed wrong, hurtful, dismissive.

Unbidden, images came to mind of how Paul's original audience might have received his words. These people embraced a religion that was thousands of years old, people who were explicitly persecuted and oppressed by the government for their ancient religious and ethnic identity. Images of Syrian refugees fleeing from ISIS came to mind. My usual missional enthusiasm gave way to a deep sadness that arose from imagining the difficulty of persons who had suffered for their religion to hear that it was not necessary for salvation after all.

The plunge into Paul's fearsome words continued. I felt as if I had fallen into the text and landed in the story on the wrong side. For if I substituted the words *the Gentiles* with current culture's version of Outsiders—everyone who is not "us," the unchurched, agnostics, spiritual but not religious, fundamentalists, and for some people the LGBTQ community, the divorced, the ones who have had abortions—Galatians took on an entirely different tone. If I replaced Paul's Judaism with Insider Christianity or "the churched," everyone who is "us," everyone who follows our tribe's rules and rituals; if I substituted Judaism with *my own favorite traditions*—icons, incense, order of evening prayer, silence, anointing oil, pilgrimage— well, now there was real trouble. Those traditions hold meaning for me, shaping my practice of prayer. I have experienced God through them.

I closed the Bible and placed it on the table where I keep my prayer resources—my altar space at home, which is for me a tradition—and considered how to live into this new awareness. I wondered what it meant for who I am and what I do. I wondered, and I prayed.

What part of the church's tradition . . . must be present for a group of Jesus-followers to constitute the church?

What part of the church's tradition, I asked myself, *must be present for a group of Jesus-followers to constitute the church?* The Spirit brought Jesus' words from Matthew 18 to mind: "Where two or three are gathered in my name, I am there among them" (v. 20).

Then I asked, But what does "in his name" really mean? Is it simply a pious phrase to close our prayers, or does it say more about the orientation of our soul? Soon I came to the question that remains the same today as for the Galatians in Paul's day: *Could it be that Jesus is found in the midst of outsiders who without our usual religious traditions nonetheless bear the gospel?*

That thought led me to Matthew 25:31-46, the parable of the sheep and goats with its disturbing pronouncement that we find Jesus in the least of these—the vulnerable, suffering, disempowered, and those at the mercy of others. We find Jesus in the all-too-human "traditions" of oppression, suffering, and need. "Yes," Jesus says through the parable. "I am found beyond the walls of the church; beyond religious programs; beyond rituals, rites, and institutions. Wherever people hunger and thirst, I hunger and thirst. I am out there with the people. I am out there with creation that groans."

God who is "out there" *with* and *in* the least of these, Jesus who is present whenever even two or three people gather in his orientation of love, trust, compassion, healing, Godwardness—this is the God I had believed in for a long time. But nothing had ever challenged my belief in light of my attachment to my *own* traditions. This Galatians moment brought forth a new set of questions.

If the God of Jesus and Paul were in fact bigger than Moses or Elijah could imagine—more expansive, more inclusive, more salvific—is that same God bigger than we Christians think God is? What does that concept imply for us today as the church struggles with its post-Christendom identity in a thoroughly pluralistic world?

Gatekeepers and Lock Pickers

But the most unsettling question for me that day was this: Why did I suddenly feel like a gatekeeper? Usually I am the person who picks the lock the gatekeeper sets in place. But through this experience of reading Galatians—rather, having Galatians read *me*, I realized that I too needed a larger vision of God. I had been schooled, for example, in a particular way of reading the Bible that I felt was really the "right" way. But how we read and interpret the Bible comes as part of our theological tradition. The thought entered my mind that my interpretive tradition of scripture had limits, and I acknowledged it as one of several responsible methods. *The canon of scripture itself comes in multiple traditions*, I reasoned, with Catholic and Orthodox versions having many more books than the Protestant Bible. Yet all these receive consideration within the realm of orthodoxy. I asked God to open my heart to greater love and discernment and to grant me wisdom as I returned to the epistle to the Galatians. I had entered what many would describe as liminal space.[7]

Paul convinced me afresh that a great tradition lies behind our traditions.

This time as I read through Galatians—both from a perspective of "outsiders" who nonetheless bear the spirit of Jesus and with the perspective of persons of our long, revered Christian traditions—it became a convicting text to me. For the very first time I actually heard and felt the epistle's impact in the way I believe its original audience did. Galatians opened my eyes and heart in a more compassionate way to the deep struggle the church now finds itself in as it is pushed to the margins of society. Day by day as I read each paragraph, wrestling and questioning, Paul convinced me afresh that a great tradition lies behind our traditions. In the words of Revelation 21:5, that great tradition is this: God in Christ is making all things new. Day by day I experienced within myself both the traditional church's grief in "forgetting what lies behind," as well as the hope of "straining forward to what lies ahead" (Phil. 3:13) in Christ Jesus. We see the great tradition most clearly in the Gospel narratives in those places where Jesus reveals characteristics of God.

Paul's vision in Galatians does not threaten the true gospel, which proclaims the tradition behind the tradition. It only threatens a church that subsumes the gospel to institutional priorities, doing so in the name of tradition. I took comfort in the Orthodox perspective on God and theology: God is mystery; we cannot know all there is to know about God. What we know now we "see in a mirror, dimly" (1 Cor. 13:12). With Martin Luther, I came to love this Galatians text anew.

Galatians, I saw, could help us Christians now as we navigate the rapid culture shifts in which we find ourselves. We can learn from Paul how to be open to the Holy Spirit who gifts and calls people to apostolic, prophetic, and evangelistic ministry that looks very different from what we in the inherited American church are used to. Rather than polarizing ourselves between "the traditional church" and the other emerging forms of church, we can learn from Paul to honor the revelation (literally "the revealing") of Jesus Christ wherever that happens, especially among marginalized people whom Jesus called "the least of these."[8] We can learn to move beyond the walls of church buildings and programs into our communities to join Jesus who is already there. We can still view the traditions of our denominations as expressions of the body of Christ, but we can exchange competitive denominationalism for robust participation in God's diverse kingdom.

Broadening Our Vision

By paying attention to how Paul helped Jewish Christians broaden their vision of God, neighbor, tradition, and mission in the first century, we Christians can broaden our vision of God, neighbor, tradition, and mission today. Paul offers wisdom to help us move beyond fearful and paralyzing questions about racial, sexual, and spiritual "otherness," which flow from our interpretation of tradition. That wisdom will help us ask a better set of questions about what it means to be a "vital church."

The church belongs to God. The church is God's idea, not ours.

Those unsettling weeks were not easy; God is the divine Disturber of the Peace. I am so grateful for God's attentive care for me as I wrestled from one chapter to the next. I know that God has that same care for the church, which makes it possible for us to wrestle together and find our way forward with wisdom and grace.

This little volume reflects on those weeks of struggling through Paul's epistle to the Galatians. This is not an exegetical tome on the epistle. It is, rather, a collection of essays that offer the missional wisdom of Paul to the church today via a reflective reading of Galatians.

I have included questions for conversation at the end of each chapter with the hope that small groups of friends may read and discuss it together. I offer this book to you, God's beloved church of the early twenty-first century, with deep gratitude for all the ways you have nurtured me and countless others in the way of Jesus. I offer it to you as an act of solidarity with your struggle to find your way when it feels as if someone has pulled the rug out from under your collective feet. And I offer it as contrition for the times when those of us who feel urgency to follow the apostolic way have been less than sensitive to your grief.

The God we love . . . is much bigger than we knew.

May the apostle Paul's fortitude and wisdom guide us as we follow the Christ who makes all things new. The God who made us loves us and will not fail us. The church belongs to God. The church is God's idea, not ours. The diverse forms of the church from one generation to the next, from one culture to the next are God's idea, not ours. Our vocation as the church involves our participation with God so that we can give this world a glimpse into God's great heart of love. To take up our apostolic vocation today we have to come to terms with this reality: The God we love, the God revealed in Christ, is much bigger than we knew. God has never been bound by our theology or our traditions. It is now time for us to see the unbound God.

For Reflection

- Where are you on the spectrum between staunch traditionalist and apostolic instigator?

- What shaped you spiritually and culturally to be where you are with spirituality and the church today?

- What excites you about reading this book?

- What worries you about reading this book?

- Read Galatians 1:1-5. As you consider Paul's commissioning to be an apostle (one sent out by God), what questions surface for you?

- If you could ask Paul one question, what would it be?

ONE

Loving the Tradition behind the Tradition

Paul an apostle—sent neither by human commission or from human authorities, but through Jesus Christ and God the Father, who raised him from the dead—and all the members of God's family who are with me, to the churches of Galatia. . . .

—GALATIANS 1:1-2

To UNDERSTAND the radical nature of Paul's letter to the Galatians, we begin with Paul's conversion. This is Paul's method: to invite the church of Galatia to the same journey of spiritual awakening that he has traversed. As he presents his own narrative of coming to know Christ, Paul cites the authority of scripture, tradition, and his experience of the risen Christ.

Note carefully: For Paul, these three sources of authority are not equal. For Paul, Jesus has ultimate authority over life, texts, and traditions—both theological and philosophical. Jesus expresses his authority through who he is and how he lives, dies, and is raised from the dead. We recognize his authority in people like Ananias, who prays for Paul's healing and baptizes him after the Damascus road encounter.[1] While Paul acknowledges the authority of the apostles who followed Jesus before his death, he emphasizes that the risen Christ has called him and speaks to him. And the risen Christ holds ultimate authority. A later chapter will focus more on the question of authority. For now suffice it to say that Paul is a mystic whose direct experience of the risen Christ transforms his life. He now gives himself completely to God's work in the world.[2]

A Reinterpretation of Tradition

In Galatians, which is one of the earliest written documents to become part of our New Testament, Paul offers the reinterpretation of his own cherished and ancient tradition, a new reading of tradition given to him by Jesus:

> I want you to know, brothers and sisters, that the gospel that was proclaimed by me is not of human origin; for I did not receive it from a human source, nor was I taught it, but I received it through a revelation of Jesus Christ (Gal. 1:12).

Throughout the letter to the Galatians, Paul refers to a dynamic relationship with the Holy Spirit, urging the church to live in the Spirit, be guided by the Spirit, bear the fruit of the Spirit. Over the years of his own pilgrimage with the risen Christ, Paul learns to listen to and cooperate with Jesus through the Holy Spirit.

But you may already be asking, "How can I know that the Holy Spirit is speaking and leading? How could Paul tell that the Spirit was guiding him? How did he *know* it was God and not his own imagination or worse yet, Satan?" We must contend with these questions if we are to open ourselves to Christ as Paul did; so in subsequent chapters we shall consider these questions at some length.

> **Over the years of his own pilgrimage with the risen Christ, Paul learns to listen to and cooperate with Jesus through the Holy Spirit.**

Most of what we know about Paul comes from the epistles he wrote. In several of them he includes autobiographical material. In Galatians 1 Paul refers to the story of his dramatic conversion recorded in Acts 9.

Paul, whose Hebrew name was Saul, was born around 5 CE, making him close to Jesus' age. He enjoyed Roman citizenship with its benefits and protection, while being born a Jew.[3] He probably came from a well-to-do family. Growing up in the ancient and prosperous city of Tarsus, he received a superb education and became an outstanding young leader among the Pharisees. People noted his zeal in defending Jewish tradition. The Pharisees, one of the three primary sects within Judaism at the time, appear frequently in the Gospel narratives. They are known as protectors of tradition, especially the scriptures. In Wesleyan terms we would refer to them as the "scriptural holiness" group within Judaism.

We first meet Paul under his Hebrew name Saul[4] in Acts 7:58, where he is present for the stoning of Stephen, the first Christian martyr: "Then they dragged him [Stephen] out of the city and began to stone him; and the witnesses laid their coats at the feet of a young man named Saul." We can imagine him standing just out of range of dust and blood, holding the executioners' garments to keep them tidy. What happens next indicates Saul's approval of the murder.

> The promise of the Father that they [the disciples] will become a global witness finally moves toward fulfillment.

A great persecution breaks out straightway after the martyrdom of Stephen, with Saul leading the way. Ironically, though Jesus has told the disciples to wait for the Holy Spirit who would empower them to be his witnesses around the world, after the Spirit comes, the disciples generally have stayed put. They are still in Jerusalem when the great persecution begins. Acts 8:3 records Saul's vengeance against the perceived threat of the new sect: "Saul was ravaging the church by entering house after house; dragging off both men and women, he committed them to prison." Scattered to many places, the persecuted disciples share the gospel as they go. The promise of the Father that they will become a global witness finally moves toward fulfillment but not in a way they would have chosen.

Saul, "breathing threats and murder against the disciples of the Lord" receives the authority to track down the scattered disciples and bring them back to Jerusalem for prosecution. (Read Acts 9:1-2.) While on his way to Damascus, Saul is suddenly confronted by the risen Christ:

> Now as he was going along and approaching Damascus, suddenly a light from heaven flashed around him. He fell to the ground and heard a voice saying to him, "Saul, Saul, why do you persecute me?" He asked, "Who are you, Lord?" The reply came, "I am Jesus, whom you are persecuting. But get up and enter the city, and you will be told what you are to do." The men who were traveling with him stood speechless because they heard the voice but saw no one. Saul got up from the ground, and though his eyes were open, he could see nothing; so they led him by the hand and brought him into Damascus. For three days he was without sight, and neither ate nor drank.
>
> Now there was a disciple in Damascus named Ananias. The Lord said to him in a vision, "Ananias." He answered, "Here I am, Lord." The Lord said to him, "Get up and go to the street called Straight, and at the house of Judas look for a man of Tarsus named Saul. At this moment he is praying, and he has seen in a vision a man named Ananias come in and lay his hands on him so that he might regain his sight." But Ananias answered, "Lord, I have heard from many about this man, how much evil he has done to your saints in Jerusalem; and here he has authority from the chief priests to bind all who invoke your name." But the Lord said to him, "Go, for he is an instrument whom I have chosen to bring my name before Gentiles and kings and before the people of Israel; I myself will show him how much he must suffer

for the sake of my name." So Ananias went and entered the house. He laid his hands on Saul and said, "Brother Saul, the Lord Jesus, who appeared to you on your way here, has sent me so that you may regain your sight and be filled with the Holy Spirit." And immediately something like scales fell from his eyes, and his sight was restored. Then he got up and was baptized, and after taking some food, he regained his strength. (Acts 9:3-19)

Saul starts preaching about Christ in Damascus immediately upon his recovery, unsurprising in light of his zealous nature. Before long his former colleagues make an attempt on his life. Never one to shrink from danger, Paul returns to Jerusalem where he finds a friend in Barnabas who welcomes him into the frightened remnant of Jesus-followers, who at this time refer to themselves as the Way. Once again Paul has to flee for his own safety. (See Acts 9:26-30.) The next time Acts mentions Paul at the close of chapter 12 and moving into chapter 13, Barnabas and Paul are commissioned to serve the church together in Antioch. During this time in Antioch, under Barnabas and Paul's leadership, Jesus' followers begin to be called Christians, a term of derision that means "little Christs."

The Damascus Road

As Paul launches into his letter to the Galatians, he describes the ego-shattering Damascus road experience. In a long passage (Gal. 1:11–2:21) he provides a detailed narrative to persuade the Galatians that he has not come into a more expansive theology without great struggle.[5]

Paul states that he was a violent man, advanced beyond others his age in his knowledge and zeal for tradition. (Apparently he follows the violent Shammaite school of thought within the larger Pharisee tradition, carrying out his duty by using any means necessary to suppress theological deviance.) He portrays himself as the ultimate defender of the faith, ruthless in his persecution of Christians.

After his conversion and the brief time in Damascus and Jerusalem, Paul journeys to the wilderness of Arabia. In his time, the wilderness was a vast geographic area southeast of Palestine and, of particular importance, the location of Mount Sinai. On Mount Sinai,

[Paul] neither rejects nor disrespects his tradition but comes to see it in a new light.

Moses had received the Law. It was one of the holiest places a devout Hebrew like Paul could go in order to listen to God and come to terms with what has happened.[6] There, over a period of time, he experiences direct revelations from Jesus.

The content of those encounters has radically changed Paul's understanding of his own Jewish tradition. He neither rejects nor disrespects his tradition but comes to see it in a new light. Non-Jews are just as beloved to God as Jews, he realizes. People need not follow all the rituals of the Hebrew tradition to experience God's love and salvation fully. Jesus the Messiah has come for *all* people. The Jews have played a special role in bringing the Messiah into the world for the whole world. All these revelations dismantle what Paul previously thought he knew about God. Paul also understands that persecution will mark his life, the same kind of trauma he once inflicted on others. In these opening chapters, Paul does not explain how the revelations were given, whether by dream, vision, a visible encounter with the risen Christ, or contemplative awareness. He simply states he received revelations from Jesus Christ.

In the rest of the epistle to the Galatians, Paul argues for the tradition behind his Hebrew tradition. The love of Christ has captured his heart. He has surrendered to Christ's authority. As a result he has given himself completely to God's mission in the world—a mission to everyone. As he says in Galatians 3:28, "There is no longer Jew or Greek, there is no longer slave or free, there is no longer male and female; for all of you are one in Christ Jesus." In this, one of the earliest texts in the canon, Paul subsumes his own tradition to the deeper, more ancient tradition of God making all things new.

> **The central focus of the Hebrew Bible involves the story of God who is calling forth and creating a people to bless the entire world.**

The tradition *behind* the tradition begins in Eden with God's promise of salvation to Adam and Eve. It moves forward with God's promise after the great flood and on to the calling of Abram and Sarai to be a blessing to the whole earth. All of that happens before the Hebrew tradition exists— long before Moses, the Exodus, or the giving of the Law. The central focus of the Hebrew Bible involves the story of God who is calling forth and creating a people to bless the entire world. Paul has become an apostle for an apostolic God, not by human choice or even his own human desire but by the call and empowerment of God.[7]

In the next chapter we will reflect more closely on Paul's direct experience of the risen Christ through the power of the Holy Spirit. We will consider reasons this kind of language and experience may seem foreign or even threatening in our mainline churches. We will think about what we fear in opening ourselves to direct encounters with God such as Paul experienced. Only then can we examine time-tested ways to discern whether a revelation or insight really does come from the Holy Spirit, and we'll begin to explore what might happen if we, like Paul, take seriously what the Holy Spirit is saying to the church today.

For Reflection

- Paul experienced a radical reorientation of faith on the Damascus road. When have you experienced a radical change of mind about who God is and what God is up to in the world? What happened that changed your mind? How did it change your life?

- As you consider a reframing of your own theological tradition with the "tradition behind the tradition," what feelings surface? Why?

- Paul went to the Arabian wilderness for three years of retreat in order to come to terms with his revelation: Jesus is the Christ for the whole world. Where do you go when you need to be with God for a sustained period of time? What practices help you listen to God?

- Read Galatians 1:6–2:10. What internal and external barriers did Paul probably have to work through in order to reach a place of confidence in his call to love and serve persons outside his inherited tradition?

- Which aspect of Paul's growing process resonates most closely with your own as you consider God's missional call and the church's current cultural challenges?

TWO

——

Opening Ourselves to God

I want you to know, brothers and sisters, that the gospel that was proclaimed by me is not of human origin; for I did not receive it from a human source, nor was I taught it, but I received it through a revelation of Jesus Christ.

—GALATIANS 1:11-12

Despite the example of Paul and many others in the Bible, leaders in the North American mainline church often scoff at claims that God speaks directly to folks today. People often cite resistance to that notion by relating an anecdote about a person who started a cult or committed a crime because allegedly "God told them to do it." Suspicion toward any claim that God speaks to people today has become the norm. This modern posture

31

creates problems on many levels, the most basic being our professed belief in and practice of prayer. Why would we pray if God never speaks? That would demote prayer to a monologue with talkative humans beseeching a silent and unresponsive God. I affirm the ground of all prayer as deep and trustful listening to God who loves and speaks and acts. Jesus asserted in John 10:27 that his sheep hear his voice.

We do not need self-protective resistance to the idea of God speaking to people. Rather, we require wise practices of discernment so that we can recognize when God speaks. Often God speaks in a quiet, internal way or through people or circumstances that ask us to notice and reflect on what we perceive. Rarely do persons hear God speak in an audible, external voice, though sometimes that occurs. Regardless of how people experience God's leading and speaking, a process to evaluate the spiritual experience remains crucial. Our Christian contemplative traditions provide such tried and true discernment practices.

The word *spirituality* no longer automatically conjures images of the occult or of the church.

Numerous seminary students have quietly confessed to me that if they spoke openly in a classroom about their mystical experiences they would lose credibility with peers or professors. Some feared they could not get through the ordination process if they spoke confidently of their own revelatory encounters with God, especially if, like Paul (or John Wesley for that matter!), they experienced God in a way that pushed the boundaries of their inherited tradition.

Though many of us Christian leaders and theologians believe God speaks to people through dreams, visions, and other spiritual experiences, sadly we often exclude these encounters from what we consider authoritative knowledge or a reliable source for faith and practice. We tend to marginalize or simply ignore these experiences.

Openness to the Holy Spirit

Our cultural dismissal of spiritual experience is a modern phenomenon that comes as a by-product of the Enlightenment, which elevated human reason as the most critical faculty of being human. In the past century some people claimed a rigidly empiricist stance to reject spiritual experience as not being scientifically verifiable, thus indefensible. Today the conversation is changing. With recent discoveries in neuroscience, the discussion about spiritual experience (specifically meditation) as a scientifically verifiable practice that impacts our living has shifted.[1] The word *spirituality* no longer automatically conjures images of the occult or of the church. Yet, even within the church, people remain deeply skeptical about those who actually hear from God.

To illustrate how far we have moved from Paul's openness to the Holy Spirit in my own United Methodist tradition, let me tell you about my cousin Jimmy.[2] The moment I met Jimmy is permanently etched into my mind. While I met him years before I entered seminary or learned the history of Methodism, this event has helped me enormously in understanding some of the challenges we now face in the church. It has to do with resistance to the God of Paul, the God who gives revelations, the God who not only listens but speaks.

Snakes, Guitar Pickers, and the Holy Ghost

My car wound around the last switchback, turned up a gravel driveway, and finally came to rest beside a shabby little house. It had been years since the paint peeled off. Now the whole structure resembled Lamb's Ear, silvery and soft around the edges. Jimmy's mom came out to greet me, her thick Kentucky accent sweet as the honeysuckle that draped the fence. I had come home to my people on my mother's side, Appalachian mountain folk who played fiddles and grew tomatoes the size of softballs. They were hardworking coal miners and flea market vendors, preachers and guitar pickers. I had lived my whole life thousands of miles from Kentucky, so now in my late twenties I stared in wonder at these newfound kin, women who had my face and men who walked like my brothers. Many of them, I learned, were Methodists. Great-Aunt Alice had donated the land and the money to build the Methodist church in that village years ago.

"Come on, Honey," Jimmy's mom said. "Come on in and set down. Jimmy will be here directly. He went out to check on his snakes."

Snakes? Wrapping my mind around this new piece of information, I sank into the sofa to wait, holding a glass of sweet tea. Sure enough, within half an hour Jimmy returned. It had been a good morning for snakes. He had six rattlers in his truck. They were for the Pentecostals, he said. Among all the other ways my people earned their living, Jimmy trapped snakes for the Pentecostals. I gingerly circled the truck while Jimmy pointed with a half-eaten sandwich. Large, angry snakes heaved and glared, their rattles beating in protest against the cages.

What strange world had I entered? Upon inquiry, my mother said that as a child she would sneak off to watch the holy rollers from the bushes, partly because of the snakes. She was willing to risk a whuppin' with a switch, the promised punishment if her mother found out where she had been. A child had no business with holy rollers or their snakes.

And for this reason Methodists long ago renounced Pentecostalism. The assumption has been that if you get mixed up with people who follow the Holy Ghost, next thing you know you'll have snakes and worse on your hands.

This position has kept uptown Methodism in its proper pew for the last hundred years, with pastors who do not sweat or shout, and members who reserve religious emotion for a good rummage sale. Good Methodists are intellectual in our faith, concerned with committee meetings and making sure that everything runs on time. We prefer that our clergy have master's degrees procured from accredited institutions. We like the word *institution* almost as much as we like *tradition.* We participate in soup kitchens and the like, but anything that smacks of what in Wesley's day was called "enthusiasm," well, no thanks.

But truthfully American Pentecostalism came out of Methodism. Snake handlers, though they fall on the extreme edge of

Pentecostalism, are cousins in the Methodist family tree. We sailed in the same genetic boat and didn't know it for most of our lives because the people who told the official family story in confirmation and membership classes didn't include the Pentecostal piece. (For more about this, see Ann Taves, *Fits, Trances and Visions: Experiencing Religion and Explaining Experience from Wesley to James.*) Pentecostalism resides in that hard-to-define realm of mysticism, which could lead to snakes. It is best left alone. But mysticism—the kind experienced by the apostle Paul that led to his new understanding of his own religious tradition—remains intrinsic to being human and to life in the Spirit. Its suppression in the Methodist Church accounts for Methodism's being in trouble today.

> **Mysticism . . . is intrinsic to being human and to life in the Spirit.**

Don't worry; I shall not argue that we need to bring in some snakes, although the image is rather lively. And we recall the story in Acts 28 where a venomous snake bites the apostle Paul and he stays robustly alive, precipitating an interesting turn of events. No, I propose that Methodism reclaim the grammar, conceptual framework, and the experience of Christian mysticism because it offers the holy fire of our tradition. Paul, Mary the mother of Jesus, Joseph the husband of Mary, and all the other apostles were mystics. They were mystics because they experienced revelations of Jesus Christ that absolutely changed their lives and the world. They recognized God's voice when God spoke. They trusted God's authority to lead them in new directions, beyond their inherited tradition.

John Wesley, the founder of Methodism, pioneered a new path because of divine direction that came through a mystical experience—his "heart was strangely warmed" when he received assurance from God that he really was a child of God. This turning point launched his astonishing ministry that, in time, became the Methodist Church. He embraced the tradition behind the tradition from apostolic necessity, breaking the rules and ordaining leaders for the New World because no one in his Anglican tradition in England would do it. Tradition behind the tradition is always primary.

Among other things, Methodism narrates the story of Christian mysticism. John Wesley's heartwarming experience launches him into powerful ministry. His brother Charles expresses the central role of mystical experience in his hymns. The brothers ground the Wesleyan vision for spreading scriptural holiness across the land in sanctification theology, the belief that we can be deeply transformed by the indwelling Holy Spirit. We receive the power to say no to sin and yes to righteousness and experience such transformation by God that we have the power to take the good news of the gospel to all the world. The Wesleyan message offers a holistic gospel that heals and redeems body,

> The Wesleyan message offers a holistic gospel that heals and redeems body, mind, spirit, relationships, institutions, and systems through the power of the Holy Spirit.

mind, spirit, relationships, institutions, and systems through the power of the Holy Spirit.

Phoebe Palmer, the mother of the nineteenth-century Holiness movement, was a Methodist lay revival preacher and theologian whose presence and ministry equaled any of the great mystics in church history. This Methodist mystic heard directly from God. Under her leadership, thousands encountered the fire of God at camp meetings, in small groups, and at church. Like Palmer, some of them experienced dreams, visions, voices, being undone. Out of those experiences they heard a call to mission, to be agents of healing and transformation to their world. Many of the social justice advances of the nineteenth century came through the ministry of holiness Methodists who had transformative encounters with God. Mysticism and mission go hand in hand in the Methodist story. Hearing from God and allowing ourselves to be transformed and sent in new directions is inherent in our tradition.

The Modern Pentecostal Movement

The beginnings of the modern Pentecostal movement emerged from Methodist holiness people who were serious about knowing God experientially and serving God holistically. The Azusa Street revival, considered the birthplace of modern Pentecostalism, began with William Seymour, an African American Methodist who in 1906 modeled racial and gender equality with his church in ways that scandalized uptown Methodists, along with the world at large. Today Pentecostalism is the fastest growing form of Christianity in the world. Unlike Pentecostalism in the United States, which has been scarred with prosperity gospel theology and scandal and an excessive focus on the gift of tongues, in the rest of the world Pentecostalism offers primarily a gospel of liberation and healing. It serves as a democratizing force that empowers women and the poor. At the heart of healthy Pentecostalism lies the belief that God speaks directly to people today in revelatory ways just as God spoke to Paul, Jesus, and many others in the Bible. Pentecostals believe what we mainline Christians state in our baptismal covenant: that God the Holy Spirit actively dwells within God's people, which results in missional outcomes in the world.

Hearing from God and allowing ourselves to be transformed and sent in new directions is inherent in our tradition.

People today hunger for spiritual experience, for an encounter with the living God. Millennials (the increasing majority of people who do not subscribe to Enlightenment prejudice against spiritual experience) long for spiritual experience mediated through symbols, metaphors, stories, art, music, and practices of prayer that help us listen deeply to God's voice. Today offers a time of unprecedented opportunity for us Methodists to reconnect with our own heritage of Christian mysticism, to reclaim the central importance of prayer and spiritual experience to the Christian life. In our own forgotten and rejected DNA we have what it will take to reconnect us with the apostolic power of God in mission. It is time for a new generation of leaders to come forth, new John Wesleys and Phoebe Palmers, who are filled with the fire of the Holy Spirit and who, like Paul, surrender their own traditions to the greater tradition of God making all things new.

Methodism emerged as an apostolic movement within the Anglican Church. It was born from the transformative spiritual experiences of men and women with the living God. The suppression of the Holy Spirit in Methodism led to the rise of the nineteenth-century Holiness movement, which gave birth to numerous smaller denominations and movements including the Church of the Nazarene, the Salvation Army, Pentecostal and non-Pentecostal Church of God, and by the early twentieth century, an extreme subset of autonomous Christian Methodist Pentecostals known for snake handling. Mysticism includes spiritual experience and remains intrinsic to human life. Without the tempering processes of wise discernment, it can lead to unbalanced and destructive practice. The mystical element of spirituality is vital to knowing and loving God and to loving and serving our neighbors. When we reclaim mysticism and place it in its rightful place in the Christian life and when we learn with Paul to listen to God, using good practices of discernment, we will find our way out of the ditch and back onto the way of Jesus.

> **Without the tempering processes of wise discernment, [mysticism] can lead to unbalanced and destructive practice.**

As the great saints and mystics would tell us, the ability to hear God and to be receptive to experiences of transformation such as Paul's Damascus road conversion go far beyond experiences for the sake of experience. Rather, openness to such experiences allows us to know and follow the God who loves us, the God who both listens and speaks. We need not suppress mystical experience in order to protect ourselves from deception; rather, we can employ a trustworthy process of discernment so that we can tell whether an experience, an insight, or direction is from God.

In the next chapter we will consider the methods that Paul used to determine whether he could trust his revelatory experience of the living Christ. We will reflect on the ways Paul's methods of discernment can help us in the church today.

For Reflection

- Have you ever experienced or witnessed Pentecostalism? Describe your experience. How did you respond?

- How can we help a historically non-Pentecostal congregation become more open to listening to and to following the Holy Spirit's lead responsibly?

- Where in your community do you sense the Holy Spirit inviting your church to pay attention?

- As you ponder an openness to the Spirit's leading that includes hearing from God in prayer, what feelings arise? What do you hope? If you acknowledge feelings of resistance or anxiety, what is it about the experience that causes these feelings?

THREE

—

Authority, Discernment, Call

Then after fourteen years I went up again to Jerusalem
with Barnabas, taking Titus along with me. I went up in
response to a revelation. Then I laid before them (though
only in a private meeting with the acknowledged leaders)
the gospel that I proclaim among the Gentiles, in order to
make sure that I was not running, or had not run, in vain.
—GALATIANS 2:1-2

As we read Paul's brief autobiographical narratives scattered
throughout his epistles, we can piece together the basis on
which he chose to trust the revelations given to him by Christ.
(We find portions of his story in Acts 9–28; 1 Corinthians 9;
Galatians 1–2; and Philippians 1–4.)

First, right after the Damascus road experience, Paul seeks the insight of those who have followed Christ longer, beginning with Ananias who baptized him, along with the Damascus Church. Soon he comes to know Barnabas, Peter, and other apostles with whom he can discuss his awakening and his call experience. He also desires their acceptance and affirmation of him as an apostle.

In seeking the wisdom of other apostles, Paul does not attribute their authority to their having a formal theological education or to their having an assigned position in a respected religious institution. They have neither of these assets. Rather, he recognizes and respects their authority because they have been with Jesus from the beginning, and the Holy Spirit fills them. Their authority flows from the same risen Christ who met Paul on the Damascus road.

Spiritual Maturity

Yet Paul does not unquestioningly follow these apostles. As Paul matures spiritually over the years, the day comes when he confronts Peter because of Peter's lapse into hypocrisy. Paul challenges other colleagues whom he sarcastically calls "super-apostles" because of their inappropriate boast and swagger. (See 2 Corinthians 11:5-6; Galatians 2:11-13.) In the case of Peter, the love of God for Jew and Gentile alike has become one of Paul's nonnegotiables for authentic Christian faith and practice. When Peter deviates from that position, Paul calls him on it. Paul rejects the super-apostles' competitive jockeying for power. He considers such behavior incompatible with Jesus' life and death and his own post-Resurrection encounters with Jesus that humbled his inflated ego. As he writes in his letter to the Philippians, the nature of Christ is that of a humble servant.

So one of the first lessons we learn from Paul as he discerns whether revelations he received were truly from Christ, thus worthy of his trust and obedience, comes in *conferring with spiritually mature people who have known Jesus (not just known about Jesus) longer than he has.* The apostles who knew Jesus prior to his death and resurrection give Paul their blessing, acceptance, and affirmation because his astonishing story corresponds with the way of the Jesus they knew.

The love of God for Jew and Gentile alike has become one of Paul's nonnegotiables for authentic Christian faith and practice.

As we traverse the culture shifts that we now face in the twenty-first century, Christ invites us to a broader vision of God and a much more diverse church than we could imagine before. The movement into what is emerging can feel chaotic and anxious. Not every emerging expression bears faithful witness to the gospel of Jesus Christ. In seeking discernment in these matters we can benefit from seeking the insight and wisdom of spiritual friends who are mature, filled with the Holy Spirit, and who model the way of Jesus in their living. In general, these individuals will be known for their wisdom, compassion, nonjudgmental presence, and deep love for God and people. The best spiritual companions for times like these are saints who do not fit well into anyone's theological box and who usually defy labels such as *conservative* or *liberal*. Like Jesus, they transcend most of the artificial boundaries we use to ignore people. These wise persons may or may not be trained spiritual directors. Either way they will help us pay attention to what God is saying and doing in our lives and embolden us to respond to God's invitation.

Another part of Paul's discernment process involved *going on pilgrimage* to a location sacred in his Jewish tradition. He does this in order to spend time in *sustained prayer*. When Paul journeys to the wilderness of Arabia, the location of Mount Sinai, he treads the same earth that Moses, Elijah, and many other heroes of his faith have walked.

God in Christ is bigger than the God Paul thought he knew.

On that holy ground he reflects on stories he first heard at his mother's knee and that shaped his Pharisaic education. He ponders the ancestors of his faith—Abraham, Sarah, Hagar. He remembers the judges, kings, and prophets; the faithful and the apostate; the famous and the obscure. The Psalms order his daily prayer as he gazes at Mount Sinai and watches the sun set over barren lands. For three long years Paul experiences the reorientation that only a pilgrimage can provide.[1]

As Paul goes on pilgrimage we can imagine his cognitive dissonance. His former interpretations of scripture and his understanding of his own Jewish traditions no longer seem adequate in light of his lived experience. The Jesus he encounters on the Damascus road is not the Messiah he and his friends have been expecting. He finds the suffering and shame heaped upon Jesus incomprehensible for those who expect a conquering king. Indeed, whenever Jesus speaks to his disciples of his impending suffering and death, they too resist him. At one point he asks if all of them will leave him. (Read John 6:66-67.)

Many details of Jesus' life and now Jesus' post-Resurrection revelations to Paul lie beyond anything Paul's former belief system could contain. What Paul sees with his own eyes, hears with his own ears, and experiences in his own body utterly contradict his former interpretation of both scripture and tradition. God in Christ is bigger than the God Paul thought he knew.

Blessedness as Reward

Many people live a clean, upright Christian life, following the rules, never missing church, and believing that they are blessed because of appropriate behavior. Though their theology may be subconscious, they believe that others receive from God exactly what they deserve as well. These folks consider being blessed a reward for being good. Then some event or experience shatters their worldview: a death in the family, a divorce, being fired, getting sick, experiencing clinical depression, having a child that makes destructive choices, falling in love with someone outside of the faith, coming out about sexuality, or some other cataclysm.

In the middle of the chaos, these "good" and richly blessed people often realize the complete inadequacy of their former vision of God, themselves, their church, and their world. They begin to see that good people suffer every kind of pain that afflicts the not-so-good. Compassion and solidarity with others who suffer in the same way they suffer comes to the fore, even if the others are not the "right" religion or have made poor moral choices. As the illusion of control over their own lives falls away, they open to the mystery of a God who is more present, more merciful, and more vulnerable than they ever imagined. "Blessed" takes on a new meaning that reflects more on suffering than success. Now space opens within their hearts and minds that allows for a much deeper relationship with God than they have ever experienced. Richard Rohr has written about this process in his book *Falling Upward: A Spirituality for the Two Halves of Life*. Paul experiences this process, beginning with the Damascus road.

Opening Space in Heart and Mind

As Paul walks and prays in the Arabian wilderness, we can easily imagine him wondering, *Did I dream those events on the Damascus road, or did they really happen? No, I could not have imagined it because there were witnesses. Every follower of the Way in Damascus knows what happened. I remember the touch of Ananias, his hands on my head, the scales falling away. Being able to see again. He came to me knowing full well I was on my way to arrest him. Such courage! And the baptism, the water, the tears. But how can this be true? Ananias is one of them, not one of us!* We can picture Paul in the Arabian wilderness going over and over his experience, holding it up against what he thought he knew about God and people. Each time he goes through it in his mind, his heart longs for surety. What his mind sees and what his heart feels will change everything. It will change his future and the future of the church. It will change the world. If he gives himself to what he now understands about God with the same zeal for God he has always felt, he will get into a lot of trouble. His life will be at risk. All these thoughts come to him as he prays, listens,

Are we living the Gospel story or living the world's story?

and remembers. In the process, Paul receives *a new interpretation of old stories.* Jesus shows him meaning that expresses the tradition behind the tradition.

Wendy Miller in *Jesus Our Spiritual Director: A Pilgrimage through the Gospels*, describes a narrative practice of discernment that she bases on a meditative reading of the Gospels.[2] By reading and praying with the stories in the Gospels, we gradually learn to live into the stories of Jesus.

"Which story are we living?" Wendy asked me in a recent conversation. "We pause from time to time, especially when we need discernment about a decision, and we need to ask ourselves: Are we living the Gospel story or living the world's story?" Narrative discernment for Wendy necessitates deep familiarity with the Gospel stories, first of all, and then learning to let the narratives speak to us in various life situations. By doing so, we increasingly incarnate Jesus' love, wisdom, and life-giving presence among our neighbors.

Wendy's Gospel narrative method of discernment always brings Jesus—the stories of his life, his actions, and his teachings—to the situation at hand. There the person attempting discernment has an opportunity not only to re-story his or her life into the Gospel story but gradually to experience Jesus' authority in interpreting scripture and life. Through this method of discernment, we begin to encounter the God who is within and behind the lives in the biblical narrative. We experience Jesus as our spiritual director.

For example, at a recent retreat Wendy invited persons to read the story of Bartimaeus in Mark 10:46-52:

> [Jesus and his disciples] came to Jericho. As he and his disciples and a large crowd were leaving Jericho, Bartimaeus son of Timaeus, a blind beggar, was sitting by the roadside. When he heard that it was Jesus of Nazareth, he began to shout out and say, "Jesus, Son of David, have mercy on me!" Many sternly ordered him to be quiet, but he cried out even more loudly, "Son of David, have mercy on me!" Jesus stood still and said, "Call him here." And they called the blind man, saying to him, "Take heart; get up, he is calling you." So throwing off his cloak, he sprang up and came to Jesus. Then Jesus said to him, "What do you want me to do for you?" The blind man said to him, My teacher, let me see again." Jesus said to him, "Go; your faith has made you well." Immediately he regained his sight and followed him on the way.

With a series of thoughtful questions, Wendy invited attendees to enter the story with their current circumstances. She asked them to imagine Jesus and the disciples passing by their home, work, or other situation where they, like Bartimaeus, felt confined or bound by a life circumstance. "Spend time now with Jesus in prayer," she urged the group. "Jesus is asking what you want him to do for you. Go ahead and tell him, and then in prayer listen and watch to see what happens next." After the time of prayer and sharing, group members encouraged one another to take the next steps Jesus had revealed in prayer. Many people found this approach to listening to Jesus transformative. Through it they encountered the Holy Spirit who is within and behind the story of Bartimaeus.

Paul's experience in the desert seems similar. The living Christ has come to him, spoken to him, called him, and sent him. Christ has given Paul authority to be an apostle to Gentiles as well as Jews. Paul sums up with finality in Galatians 2:19-21 that he has died to his former life and risen to a new life that he completely identifies with Christ: "I have been crucified with Christ; and it is no longer I who live, but it is Christ who lives in me. And the life I now live in the flesh I live by faith in the Son of God, who loved me and gave himself for me."

Jesus is asking what you want him to do for you. Go ahead and tell him, and then in prayer listen and watch to see what happens next.

We could argue that the claim that "God spoke to me and said to do thus and so" is too subjective. But, in the end, the character of a person and the fruit of a person's life support the reality of a divine commission. Paul's extraordinary ministry continues to bear fruit two millennia later. Clearly his call and revelations from Christ were real.

The same Christ who stopped Paul on the Damascus road, who spoke to Paul directly in the Arabian wilderness and beyond, calls and speaks to us today. We can trust the wisdom and direction Christ gives us, just as Paul did, using reliable means of discernment. Indeed, if we are to be a lively and fruit-ful church in the future, this is the only way it will happen.

For Reflection

- To whom do you turn when you need clear-sightedness in making a decision? Who are the wise and mature saints in your life? Are there trained spiritual directors in your community who could companion you or others through discernment?

- As you consider the culture shifts that are causing the church to question the exclusion or subordination of persons based on race, gender, economic status, or sexuality, who in your life can help you explore these issues with wisdom and grace?

- Have you ever participated in a pilgrimage? If so, where did you go and what did you experience? How did you encounter God?

- What does it mean to you personally to "re-story" your life into the Gospel narratives?

- If possible, describe a time in your life when a Gospel narrative helped you to "re-story" your life.

FOUR

When Systems Change

As many of you as were baptized into Christ have clothed yourselves with Christ. There is no longer Jew or Greek, there is no longer slave or free, there is no longer male and female; for all of you are one in Christ Jesus. And if you belong to Christ, then you are Abraham's offspring, heirs according to the promise.
—GALATIANS 3:27-29

Paul's revolutionary words reflect the core wisdom Christ gave him in the Arabian desert. That time became liminal space, a threshold between what he thought he knew about God and his new realization in which he had to relearn who God is and what God is up to. The core of his new learning has to do with the equality of all people in God's eyes. Because of Christ, because of the Holy Spirit, according to the will of

God, all people receive God's salvation. Men, women, young, old, Jew, Greek, slave or free are united to Christ and therefore join him as offspring of Abraham. All "are one in Christ Jesus" and can be filled with the Holy Spirit. All can minister using the gifts of the Spirit. For a zealous young Pharisee steeped in religious and political systems that were riddled with inequality based on ethnicity, religion, gender, social strata, and more, the radical nature of Paul's words cannot be overstated.

The church in our day finds itself in equally radical liminal space. Culture shifts challenge us to become much more multicultural and egalitarian, to embody the revolutionary inclusiveness of Galatians 3:27-29 in ways that the church has yet to realize fully. When truly lived out, this text could return moral authority to the church—moral authority all but lost due to sexual misconduct, greed, sexism, racism, and other sins done in the name of God. Indeed, unless the church embraces and lives into Paul's words in this text, we will lose credibility with our neighbors, and it will be our own fault.

New Expressions of Christian Community

The emergence of today's new expressions of Christian community reflect in myriad ways the embodiment of Galatians 3:27-29. In a democratizing move that characterizes the flattening of social structures in culture at large, these faith communities are led by all sorts of people and are open to all sorts of people in ways that were virtually unheard of before now. Rev. Nadia Bolz-Weber is an Evangelical Lutheran Church of America pastor. She and her congregation exemplify this change. Rev.

Bolz-Weber's body is covered with tattoos. She speaks openly of being a recovering addict, is female, and has thousands of post-religious followers because of her snarky, irreverent, in-your-face style. Yet she values the deep tradition of the sacraments, the creeds, and the tradition behind the tradition. She wears a clerical collar. Her Denver congregation, House for All Sinners and Saints, boasts the acronym HFASS (Half Ass). Gay, straight, trans, bi, rich, poor, Republican, Democrat, and every color of people (and hair) populate this church.[1]

Culture shifts challenge us to become much more multicultural and egalitarian.

This church celebrates every kind of diversity, which characterizes the rising tide of emergence Christianity. This diversity includes forms of gatherings and locations of gatherings that defy containment in a church building on Sunday morning. Gatherings may or may not include a worship service, though worship matters greatly to emergence Christians.

The very notion of certain requirements for church to be church has come under scrutiny. For emergence Christians, community life—life together—constitutes the most important aspect. Worship, while essential, is only one facet of church.

We are in a full-blown systems change in how we think about and practice being the church. In our time, the inherited church faces decline, and new forms of church are emerging. In addition to being diverse, emergence Christian communities tend to be smaller, less ambitious, more fluid, and consciously distant from exploitative and imperialistic forms of church.

They are critical of inherited forms of church that are consumeristic and narcissistic.

Emergence Christians, as a rule, desire to practice hospitality and humility toward their neighbors as primary forms of Christian witness, eschewing any form of exploitative or gimmicky evangelism. They tend toward a kingdom of God orientation based on Luke 10 and other texts, working to discover God's activity in the neighborhood and to join in. While they believe that they are bringing Jesus *to* the neighborhood, they are also meeting Jesus *in* the neighborhood. This posture differs from the insider/outsider mind-set that is common in the inherited church. And while they welcome people into their gatherings, they do not believe that the goal of loving neighbor is to colonize them culturally. They take seriously the simple words of Jesus about God loving both the just and the unjust and sending rain on both the just and the unjust. They choose to give up all forms of control, manipulation, and colonization in the name of evangelism and mission.

> **Reformers are prophets and because their truth-telling names the need for institutional change; they can serve as lightning rods for everyone's anxiety.**

Emergence communities vary in size, structure, theological foci, and sustainability. Many new church starts of the emergence type fail. This is to be expected and, believe it or not, to be seen as a good thing. As is always the case during times of systems change, much experimentation is called for, with a high rate of failure along the way to discovering what forms of Christian community will help the church thrive into its God-given vocation in the future. I think of this healthy process as failing our way forward.

Some emergence Christians and their communities have left or been driven out of the institutional church that birthed them. That is nothing new; the same thing happened with Protestant reformations, during the rise of Methodism and during the nineteenth-century American Holiness movement, among others. Reformers are prophets and because their truth-telling names the need for institutional change; they can serve as lightning rods for everyone's anxiety. Nonetheless, several notable movements within emergence Christianity remain firmly and intentionally connected within the inherited church. These movements are impacting the church's imagination positively. I refer to the stance of these movements as "connected emergence." Richard Rohr calls it "living on the edge of the inside of both church and society," explaining that this posture is utterly Franciscan.[2]

The purpose of remaining connected while modeling emergence Christianity is twofold: to ignite renewal within the declining church and to help the emergence communities remain accountable to the "tradition behind the tradition" that the inherited church carried forward. Levels of accountability differ widely from one connected emergence community to another. The process of determining what connection looks like can be confusing, anxiety provoking, and messy both for the innovators and for the inherited church.

Fresh Expressions, a global movement that began in England among Anglicans, is one manifestation of "connected emergence."[3] The Missional Wisdom Foundation's network of missional and new monastic learning communities that started in The United Methodist Church and now resources multiple denominations across the United States and around the world is another.[4] The New Monasticism is an ecumenical, grassroots, global stream within "connected emergence" Christianity.[5]

Connected Emergence

Connected emergence operates on the assumption that institutions are not inherently bad.[6] Institutions are necessary because they form to promote and protect the core values and purpose of the people—the movement that gives birth to the institution. But over time institutions inevitably become rigid and inwardly focused, entombing the life they are meant to protect. When that happens, innovators within the institutions begin to appear. These pioneers create new expressions of the life that formerly gave birth to the institution.

A few pioneers play a God-given role of speaking truthfully to the institution about current reality so the institution can take responsibility for decline and open itself to positive change. Other pioneers play a unique role in inviting people within the declining system to come and see real examples of future possibility. In New Testament language these innovators, truth-tellers, and come-and-see people are apostles, prophets, and evangelists, respectively. Alan Hirsch in his book *The Forgotten Ways: Reactivating the Missional Church* describes the need for the declining church to reclaim the gifts of apostles, prophets, and evangelists in order to bring forth renewed missional focus.

At first only a tiny number of early adapters within the institution understand what is needed to carry the life forward, and they quickly get on board. Through their influence, a few more people join in the pioneering experiment. Once enough of the new experiments are stable and lively, larger numbers of people welcome the pioneering work. The usual figure cited as a tipping point for institutional change comes when 20 percent of the members participate in the "new" thing. Certain leaders of the declining system who have the capacity to see both the irreversible decline of what has been and the emergence of what is coming play a critical role in both tending

Over time institutions inevitably become rigid and inwardly focused, entombing the very life they are meant to protect.

the people of the declining system and protecting and nurturing the pioneers who lead the way forward. This messy and often chaotic process is the way systems change. It is crucial that a few institutional leaders maintain nonanxious presence and leadership through this process, both tending the people who won't make it into the adaptation and protecting and providing resources and blessing to the pioneers who are opening the path for what is emerging.

We in the church find ourselves in the middle of a deep systems change, the magnitude of which has only occurred three or four times in the church's history.[6] As was the case with the gospel movement launched by Jesus and with Paul's major shift to welcome Gentiles as members of God's household, our challenge is both theological and practical. The ecclesiology (what we understand church to mean) and missiology (how we bear the gospel into the world) of colonization that came to us with our inherited church are no longer tenable. *Evangelism* and *mission* have become dirty words for many Christians because of their association with everything from unscrupulous television evangelists to the genocide of First People, Native Americans, and Aboriginal and Indigenous people in many places. Church functioning as an empire that colonizes the world or as a consumer industry with customers to attract and keep is failing fast and not a moment too soon. Both of those forms of church pervert the gospel and have harmed many people.

Today we must learn from voices of those who suffered the most from domination masked as mission.

Not all evangelism and mission of the modern church has functioned in exploitative or consumeristic ways, nor have all expressions of church in the past functioned in exploitative and imperialistic ways. But those two dominant systems of church are collapsing, and to the degree that the church has been based in those systems, the church is also falling apart.

Today we must learn from voices of those who suffered the most from domination masked as mission, such as the late Richard Twiss, cofounder of the North American Institute of Indigenous Theological Studies. Dr. Twiss, a Lakota theologian whose recent *Rescuing the Gospel from the Cowboys: A Native American Expression of the Jesus Way*, provides a good introduction to an evangelical, postcolonial vision of both church and evangelism.[7]

The Question of Authority

As Phyllis Tickle described in her book *The Great Emergence: How Christianity Is Changing and Why*, during times of massive culture shifts, the question of authority comes to the forefront.[8] Who or what will become the authority in the new reality? Paul claimed the authority of Jesus Christ, given to him through revelation, over the authority of tradition. Martin Luther and other leaders of the Protestant Reformation claimed the authority of scripture over the authority of the pope.

What source of authority is now coming to the forefront in *our* time of emergence? Increasingly, authority now flows from practitioners who share hard-won wisdom through informal networks of virtual and real communities rather than from theoreticians who bring expertise in particular fields. Google, YouTube and Wikipedia have become the go-to sources for information on every topic. Some persons who supply the articles or videos found in these sources have graduate degrees, but just as often they are ordinary people who have figured out a way to solve a problem.

The turn to practitioners for wisdom comes as part of the larger turn toward experience as a valid source of knowledge. It also represents part of the flattening of the world, to borrow a phrase from Thomas L. Friedman, author of *The World Is Flat: A Brief History of the Twenty-first Century*. The ready access to endless knowledge through the Internet has changed everything, bringing widespread political, economic, and religious ramifications. Connected to and emerging from the general flattening of the world is growing resistance to rigid hierarchies of power in the church. As we move further into emergence Christianity, the church will wrestle increasingly with questions about authority, particularly with regard to who is ordained, why they are ordained, and what it means to empower the ministry of the laity.

As we move further into emergence Christianity, the church will wrestle increasingly with questions about authority.

As with Paul's religious context of Judaism and wider multicultural context of the Roman Empire, our context is both religious (Christianity as well as other religions) and political, with globalization and the emergence of transnational corporations functioning as the new, powerful "nations." The church faces multifaceted challenges that can overwhelm us with what it will require to understand our culture and be ready to engage it winsomely and authentically with the gospel. In the next chapter we will consider how to move forward faithfully as the Spirit leads, while still responding to anxiety in the system.

For Reflection

- In what ways have you noticed an increased flattening in culture, especially with regard to accessibility to information and the way that organizations function?

- Where have you noticed public resistance to top-down thinking in culture—locally, nationally, and worldwide?

- How has the advent of Google, YouTube, and Wikipedia made an impact on you personally?

- In your own context, who would you describe as an apostle, prophet, or evangelist according to this chapter's definitions?

- What will help the declining church come to grips with the culture shifts it is experiencing and enable the church to move forward as the Spirit calls?

- How can we protect the tradition behind the tradition while experimenting with new forms of Christian faith communities?

FIVE

Responding to Anxiety in the System

When the fullness of time had come, God sent his Son, born of a woman, born under the law, in order to redeem those who were under the law, so that we might receive adoption as children. And because you are children, God has sent the Spirit of his Son into our hearts, crying, "Abba! Father!"

—GALATIANS 4:4-6

As systems begin to change, anxiety mounts. Everyone within the system can feel it: a growing sense of descent into chaos. Because people cannot see where this chaos is leading, they tend to regress to familiar but counterproductive behaviors. These behaviors are meant to stop the anxiety rather than address the underlying issue. Usually the behaviors include attempts to scapegoat agents of change. (This explains why prophets are without honor in their hometown, as Jesus says in Luke 4:24!) Only a few rare leaders can remain centered and integrated enough to withstand systems change anxiety, refuse to participate in scapegoating, tend to people within the system who will not change, protect necessary space for change to happen, nurture the pioneers who are leading the way forward, and attend to all these duties in loving and wise ways. As we'll see in a moment, the chaos of systems change is not the enemy. The real problem resides in a particular type of fear, a pattern evident in the unfolding of Galatians 4.

Spiritual Confusion

The ancestral religious practices of the Galatians (who were the original Celts) included a belief in elemental spiritual powers found in earth, air, water, and fire. Some scholars believe Paul refers to these elemental spirits in Galatians 4:3 when he reminds them of the spiritual bondage from which they are freed: "We were enslaved to the elemental spirits of the world." From there Paul proceeds to make a strong and complex argument as to why they must not allow themselves to be taken captive again now that they are free in Christ. He summarizes in Galatians 5:1: "For freedom Christ has set us free. Stand firm, therefore, and do not submit again to a yoke of slavery."

Yet the most worrisome worldview Paul addresses in this epistle is not Celtic beliefs in earth, air, water and fire. His use of "we" suggests he is talking about another matter—an appealing aspect from another religious tradition that threatens to derail the Galatians from their freedom in Christ. Paul's concern centers on spiritual confusion caused by a group of Jewish Christians who have come among the Galatians whom Paul **Only a few rare** has already evangelized. The new **leaders can** group teaches that Gentiles have **remain centered** to follow all Jewish traditions **and integrated** (including circumcision of males) **enough to** in order to become followers of **withstand** Jesus. Possibly Paul refers to these **systems change** "Judaizing" teachings as "elemen- **anxiety.** tal spirits," metaphorically using a phrase familiar to the Galatians in order to help them understand the danger of losing their way. "You foolish Galatians!" he cries earlier in 3:1. "Who has bewitched you?"

At the time Paul writes Galatians these "elemental spirits" teachers have so influenced the people that they now observe many Jewish rituals, festivals, and other practices, hoping to retain God's favor. Paul's distress at the damage being done is evidenced in his anguished, maternal language:

> I am afraid that my work for you may have been wasted. . . . My little children, for whom I am again in the pain of childbirth until Christ is formed in you, I wish I were present with you now and could change my tone, for I am perplexed about you. (Gal. 4:11, 19-20)

Why would other Christian missionaries follow Paul around and "mess with" the young churches? What would

motivate such behavior? Paul himself suggests egotistical
motives, though he does not use the word *ego*. The interlop-
ers use exclusionary tactics against the Galatians in order to
gain power over the church:

Fear can make the best of us act our worst. "They make much of you, but for no good purpose; they want to exclude you, so that you may make much of them" (Gal. 4:17).

Their motive may be self-aggrandizement, but I suspect that it
has much to do with fear. And fear can make the best of us act
our worst.

When we experience anxiety, most of us simply want to
make it go away. It is an unpleasant feeling. We connect our
earliest experiences of anxiety with needing a parent to hold
us, feed us, and tend to our basic human needs. These survival
connections with anxiety multiply exponentially when we have
experienced trauma, abandonment, or other painful events.
Often our unfinished business from long ago surfaces when
anxiety enters the systems in which we live, work, and worship.
In spiritual direction or therapy we may discover that a good
deal of our anxiety during systems change is more about our
family of origin than about the situation at hand. The exponential character of anxiety can make us feel as if anxiety were the
urgent problem we must address. So we hurriedly make choices
out of fear and discomfort—not to address the current situation
but to relieve our anxiety. Since change seems to be causing the
anxiety, the knee-jerk response is to stop change so the anxiety
will end.

Yet the source of the problem is not anxiety. Therapists encourage anxious clients to "sit" with their anxiety so as to make decisions out of freedom rather than fear. A big part of the therapeutic task comes in helping clients recognize what triggers their anxiety and why. Our conviction that we are deeply loved and that God will not abandon us provides a path for us to move through anxiety. We acknowledge God's presence with us at an emotional level while in the anxiety-producing event. The capacity to *respond* instead of *react* to anxiety-provoking events has much to do with our general sense of security.

As persons sit with their anxiety and reflect mindfully on their belovedness, internal space opens for awareness of the source of their anxiety. So much of our anxiety comes back to our sense of identity, our need for security, and our need to belong. From a stance of belovedness we can recognize when these legitimate human needs feel threatened by change, and we can trace out the root cause of old anxiety that has surfaced. We can choose life-giving responses that we base on our trust in God and openness to God's work in the world. We can become compassionate toward others who are stuck, and we can become courageous to make necessary change.

Often our unfinished business from long ago surfaces when anxiety enters the systems in which we live, work, and worship.

As Paul moves into his discourse in chapter 4 about true and false teaching, he reminds the church of its authentic status with God. Those within the church can rely on the fact that God is now Abba for them—a loving parent. God is *with* them and *for* them (4:4-7). They are beloved to God. The Spirit of Jesus resides in them, crying "Abba" or "Papa" in their hearts. They can trust this love. Their familial relationship with God provides the essential grounding to recognize true and reliable teaching.

Sarah and Hagar

Using an allegorical reference that often confuses readers today, Paul draws from a familiar biblical story of Sarah and Hagar. (Read Genesis 16–22.) This rabbinic literary move is common in ancient Jewish biblical interpretation. (Notice that Paul is not a biblical literalist.) Paul uses Hagar's story as an allegorical representation of religion based on Jewish law and its rituals. The logic goes like this: Sarah decides that her servant Hagar will be the surrogate for a long-awaited son. God has promised Sarah that she will bear a son, but it is taking too long and she has lost hope. Hagar serves as Sarah's Plan B. Thus the Hagar narrative (that is, "Hagar" in Galatians 4) represents our efforts to secure God's promise and blessing by our own methods, especially through following religious rituals.

Sarah's narrative of giving birth to Isaac, on the other hand, represents religion based on God's promise and gift in Christ. Paul calls this path "Sarah." Paul names the preferred path "Sarah" because, despite Sarah's mistakes and failures along the way, in due time God does come through, and Sarah gives birth to Isaac. Isaac is sheer gift to Sarah and Abraham. Due to their age, they could do nothing in their human power to conceive.

The allegorical choice of Sarah's story represents salvation as the gift of God through Christ rather than salvation earned through human effort. An important aspect to remember about Paul's complicated argument is that the story of Abraham and Sarah takes place many hundreds of years before a Hebrew people exists, much less the Jewish law. This deliberate choice on Paul's part reinforces his central thesis that we are not saved by

> We wrap our identity, security, and belonging in the narratives we believe about our community and ourselves.

being Jewish and following the law but by the work of Christ, which is a gift for all people.

Paul's arguments in Galatians 4 can seem obscure to contemporary readers. However, some elements of Paul's method provide deep wisdom for us in our interpretive work around systems change. We wrap our identity, security, and belonging in the narratives we believe about our community and ourselves. The anxiety of systems change always taps into deeper fears related to identity, security, and belonging. Paul's genius in referring to both Celtic religious language about "elemental spirits" and allegorical readings of Genesis comes in his framing the massive paradigm shift with stories and language familiar to both his Jewish and Gentile audiences. In doing so he also reframes the meaning of the old stories to call attention to God's intention toward the world. That is, he reminds them of the tradition behind the tradition, and that tradition has *everything* to do with their identity, security, and belonging.

At this point let us return to the earlier question as to why other Jewish Christians would consciously undermine Paul's apostolic work. Paul names self-centered motives as the likely culprit. Those teachers want to displace Paul and his theology with their own theology and authority. They desire power over the Galatian church. Could it be, though, that these "Judaizers" are reacting to anxiety in the changing system? Do they feel threatened in their sense of identity, security, or belonging by this strange new doctrine that Gentiles can be saved without becoming Jews? After all, controlling, self-centered behaviors usually emerge from fear.

> [The contemplative congregation] will also attract people who want to be part of a community that brings transformation to a broken world.

So what are we to do in the face of all this anxiety? The solution, while not quick or easy, is simple. We must lead our communities of faith into a contemplative stance, helping them to reorient themselves as the beloved children of God. We must systematically and repeatedly introduce them to practices of prayer that encourage listening to help them soak in God's love. We must teach them the practice of *lectio divina*, which in John Wesley's terminology was called "searching the Scriptures." We must encourage them to pray regularly using a prayer of examen so that they begin to recognize, habitually, what is life-giving and what is death-dealing not just in their personal lives but in the life of the church.[1] We must help congregations move into this stance so that they can recognize and respond trustingly to the Holy Spirit's leadership.

I realize that I have used the word *must* more times than allowable in one paragraph, yet I have done this deliberately. No other way exists for us to move from fear to faith. Making that shift requires intentionality. Fortunately we have thousands of years of wisdom at our service through the voices and practices of saints who learned to listen to God, move with God, and love well. The forms of prayer I enumerate above come from the long, ancient tradition of the church.

Guiding a church into a contemplative stance requires modeling on the part of clergy and lay leaders.

The process of helping a congregation move into a contemplative stance can take several years; not everyone can make the shift. Some people will angrily leave the church when they realize they cannot seize control. Others will adapt gratefully to the new direction. Most people will take some time. As the congregation enters a contemplative stance, it will attract people who desire spiritual depth and wisdom for life in their church home. It will also attract people who want to be part of a community that brings transformation to a broken world.

Guiding a church into a contemplative stance requires modeling on the part of clergy leaders and lay leaders as well as intentionality in everything the church does—from planning the flow of worship to shaping the way leadership meetings are run. Intentional shepherding into a contemplative stance offers the best way to help an anxious congregation come to trust deeply in the assurance of verse 5 of Psalm 23: God prepares a table for us in the presence of all that we fear.

My understanding of the contemplative stance includes this fourfold practice:

1. Show up to God, ourselves, our neighbors, and our world.
2. Pay attention to what is there, what is going on inside and outside of ourselves.
3. Cooperate with God as God invites, instructs, corrects, or encourages in the situation at hand.
4. Release the outcome of cooperation with God. Consciously let go of the outcome, recognizing that God is God and we are not.

As congregations become habituated to this fourfold practice of a contemplative stance, they will learn to respond to systems change from a position of belovedness and inner freedom rather than fear.[2] Being grounded in solid practices of discernment as a result of the fourfold contemplative stance allows congregations to chart a course through times of culture shift. And one side effect of their grounding in God's love is that the church will become more attractive to those neighbors who long for a spiritual community where wisdom and love prevail.

For Reflection

- In your family of origin how did your family members handle anxiety? What triggered anxiety for the family as a whole, and how did you learn to respond?

- In your congregation, in what ways have you encountered anxiety over systems change? How do people in your congregation typically react or respond to anxiety related to systems change?

- Who are the lay leaders, clergy, and judicatory leaders in your area who seem to display the vision and gifts of "both/and" leadership: tending persons in the declining system while making space, protecting, and blessing the innovators who lead necessary change? How can you and your congregation support these leaders in practical ways?

- How could you encourage your congregation to move into a contemplative stance as described in this chapter?

- Of the practices of the fourfold contemplative stance, which do you find most natural? Why? Which challenges you most? Why?

- Imagine incorporating the contemplative stance into a church setting such as a leadership meeting. How would the stance be introduced? How might it shape the way the meeting unfolded? What do you imagine would be the resistance to this shift? How could the resistance be heard and processed in a healthy way without allowing it to derail the shift?

SIX

———

Guided by the Spirit

If we live by the Spirit, let us also be guided by the Spirit.
—Galatians 5:25

In the last chapter we considered the importance of living into a contemplative stance as communities of faith. Without this orientation we will find it difficult to recognize what the Spirit is saying to the church, much less have the will to cooperate with what God is doing during systems change. In this chapter we will move with Paul into a consideration of nimble, day-by-day following of the Holy Spirit as communities of faith. As Paul stresses emphatically, the whole point of freedom in Christ is so that the Spirit can guide us.

Having made his argument for choosing the path of Sarah (faith and freedom in Christ) in Galatians 4, Paul in chapter 5 sharply contrasts living in freedom for God's sake with using freedom from the law as an excuse for selfishness. It is crucial that we not underestimate our sinful capacity to use religion as a tool. In this chapter we will look at taking responsibility for our bad behavior during systems change.

As Paul enumerates various expressions of selfishness, which he collectively calls "the flesh," it is no surprise to see drunkenness, sorcery, or licentiousness on the list. What requires our attention on this laundry list of sin—for the discussion at hand—are the communal "works of the flesh" that sprout like mushrooms during times of systems change. Sandwiched among groups of individualistic sins, seven toxic attitudes and actions that thrive in a climate of anxiety are named: "enmities, strife, jealousy, anger, quarrels, dissensions, factions" (Gal. 5:20). They are infectious and toxic to the mission of God's church.

Tradition in most of these cases means "the way we do things around here."

We face all these destructive attitudes and actions during shifts in the balance of power in the church. Each reaction displays lack of trust in God's love and presence and lack of security in our identity as God's children. These sins judge others whose lives, ministries, or perspectives do not put us and our comfort at the center of the universe. As we indulge the urge to ignite jealousy in our little group toward the group that is leading change; as we form a faction, feed dissension, try to discredit the innovators, we also unleash shame in ourselves.

We acknowledge our attitudes and actions as harmful—ones that can divide or kill the church. Even more, we know our behavior does not reflect who we really are. Often at this point, people leave the church. They feel disgusted with the church, unable to stop the change, and unhappy with themselves.

Others stay but do even more damage by resisting change in the name of doing what is right. We easily mask a "fleshly" drive for control with pious language about tradition. Usually church people who resist the change that God is inviting, do so in the name of protecting tradition. But they are not thinking about the tradition behind the tradition, nor are they usually oriented outwardly in their concept of church. The notion of God as a God on the move (God is more about tents than temples) does not fall within their concept of tradition nor a missional God within their imagination. Tradition in most of these cases means "the way we do things around here." Even if the way things have always been done no longer works, the thought of change triggers deeper anxiety than the slow disintegration that is underway.

Fear or anger does not promote creative or playful thought about change. Feelings of threat propel us instinctively to fight-or-flight mode. We cannot exercise wise discernment when controlled by visceral emotions. Our bodies override thoughtful, nuanced reflection and demand that we either fight the enemy or flee for our lives.

As you can imagine, this overriding of thoughtful reflection presents a dilemma of multiple dimensions. Persons caught in this situation face deep uncertainties about what kind of god God is, who has power and who should and should not have power, the nature of the church, and countless memories of and attachments to the way things used to be. Many of you who are reading this book will recognize this scenario all too well. Some of the worst behavior I have witnessed in the church has occurred in this situation. So how do we as leaders head off this problem before it happens? Or if we are leading a congregation experiencing this kind of anxiety, what can we do?

In his magnum opus, *A Failure of Nerve: Leadership in the Age of the Quick Fix*, Dr. Edwin H. Friedman discusses the importance of the "differentiated leader," the kind of leader necessary to guide a congregation through deep systems change.[1] Differentiated leaders are aware of the cause of the anxious system and the need for change. They acknowledge and tend to their unfinished business. Without good self-care, leaders of anxious congregations can unwittingly participate in projection, transference, or scapegoating in order to relieve personal anxiety. Differentiated leaders remain a peaceful, nonanxious presence while overseeing change, thus over time shifting the group dynamic of the system toward a healthier stance.

Leading from a Contemplative Stance

Moving from Friedman's language to the framework of Christian spirituality discussed in Galatians 5, we discover that differentiated leaders take a contemplative stance. At risk of redundancy, let's remember what that means for leaders. Contemplative leaders show up to self, others, and God. They pay attention to what is going on within themselves as well as within and beyond their congregations. These leaders notice what God is doing in their own lives and outwardly in the congregation, as well as in the community beyond the walls of the church. They are conscious of their own resistance to God's invitation, and they work through it. This gives them discernment and spiritual authority to recognize and speak to congregational resistance to the Spirit. The contemplative leader lives and acts out of this deep attentiveness, following the guidance of the Holy Spirit and releasing the outcome of that obedience to God. Contemplative leaders exhibit profound courage and inner freedom. They are present, compassionate, discerning, wise, and resilient. They love well.

All of that to say this: If we as leaders are now positioned to lead the church through systems change, we have to work on our own unfinished business. We **Contemplative leaders show up to self, others, and God.** cannot assume we have already taken care of it. Our inner work is never finished. This work requires that we be persons of listening prayer. We need a support network to help us stay right side up because the anxiety of systems change will bring all our unresolved issues and unhealed wounds to the surface. A spiritual director, possibly a therapist, and a small number of trusted friends are essential.

We choose well by following Paul's example as he leads the Galatians through a paradigm shift. He helps them reconnect to the tradition behind the tradition. We must also foster reconnection to the tradition behind the tradition. Teaching is a key component of leading the church through systems change.

When it comes to teaching the church about honoring the real tradition, we can begin with a story from the origins of our church to provide definitions of words and concepts that will build a strong foundation for leading change. Remember, for example, that the Latin word *traditio*, whence *tradition* comes, means "to hand on for safekeeping," a definition everyone needs to know. Then we can talk about what exactly should be handed on and why. Narratives about the original spiritual community pass down in a powerful way the tradition behind the tradition and thereby follow Paul's example.

The goal of these preliminary investigations with our congregations is to probe questions such as these while exploring well-chosen stories from our church tradition:

- What is the meaning of "tradition"? What is the value of having traditions?

- What today do we need to hand on for safekeeping?

- What original energy undergirded the planting of our church/denomination/theological movement?

- Why did John Wesley/Martin Luther/John Calvin/ Menno Simons begin renewal movements? What DNA did they hope to recover?

- What does the long tradition that we now feel obliged to protect and hand on involve? the arrangement of furniture in the sanctuary? the organ, piano, or keyboard? traditional worship versus contemporary? a particular way of doing children's ministry? Is it the church's involvement at the soup kitchen? the local elementary school? the softball league?

- What do we mean when we speak of the tradition that we must hand on?

Through stories of the founding of our church or denomination, we can highlight what motivated people like John Wesley to launch what became the Methodist movement. He desired to reclaim the tradition behind the tradition of God making all things new. We can trace through the history of our church or denomination how that DNA has been expressed in multiple ways over the years, and we can remember other times in the past when we have moved through systems change. Link these times of remembering to solid teaching and preaching from the pulpit and to small-group study to help the church reconnect scripturally with the missional God.

The intent of this book, *God Unbound*, is to help with that process in relation to scripture. In addition to Galatians, use Luke 10 and the book of Acts as narrative-rich New Testament texts. The powerful ancestral narratives of the first five books of the Bible, particularly the call of Abram and Sarai, also offer solid grounding. Paul refers to their call when he leads the Galatians through systems change.

When God calls Abram and Sarai in Genesis 12:1-3, God issues a mission to launch a new kind of people who will become a blessing to the whole world. In time Isaac's birth sets in motion the promise's fulfillment. God makes it clear from the start that the divine intent is to bless all families of earth, not just the bloodline of Abram and Sarai. This story initiates the understanding that God is a missional God who calls forth a missional people in order to bring about the healing and salvation of the world. This story gives voice to the great and unchanging tradition that we are to hand on: God is always calling forth a people to participate in God's work of making all things new. We must evaluate all our little traditions in light of this, the great tradition.

Luke 10:1-24 presents Jesus sending out seventy disciples in pairs to take the message of the kingdom of God to all who will receive it. One striking aspect: The disciples are to travel and serve in vulnerability rather than power. They will depend upon the hospitality of those they meet. When they face resistance, their nonviolent response is to shake the dust of inhospitality off their shoes. They release the outcome to God. They offer people they meet the message that the kingdom of God has come. Jesus sends them to all the places he plans to visit. They serve as his ambassadors, preparing the way.

Through careful reading, reflection, and prayer, leaders can help a congregation live into this Gospel story, which carries forward through Jesus and his disciples the tradition behind the tradition. This narrative can become a mirror to help a congregation reflect on its current practices in light of the missional practice of Jesus with his original disciples.

Through reading and studying the book of Acts, congregations can reconnect with the wondrous story of Pentecost, the birth of the church, and the ways in which ordinary Christians became gospel bearers throughout the Roman Empire. They will meet Saul the Pharisee who becomes Paul the apostle and journey with the other church planters as the church multiplies in different contexts. These stories can mirror what is important to the local church and what changes need to be made.

Take all these journeys through key scriptural narratives with attentiveness to the following:

- the denomination's founding story, including the apostolic vision of the founder(s)

- the congregation's founding story, including the apostolic vision of the founding pastor(s) and congregation

- the neighborhood in which the church exists—its founding story, its history in relationship to the church, and its current reality

In this process of helping the congregation remember its own origin in the tradition behind the tradition, Paul's words in Galatians 5:6 take on particular significance: "For in Christ Jesus neither circumcision nor uncircumcision counts for anything; the only thing that counts is faith working through love." In the context of systems change, we could paraphrase Paul's words in this way: "For in Christ Jesus neither handbells nor praise bands count for anything" or "neither church buildings nor lack of church buildings count for anything." Whatever the small *t* tradition happens to be, whatever the emerging expression of church happens to be, the only aspect that counts in the long run is faith working through love. We learn to recognize temptation to bad behavior that can surface during systems change. With God's help we take responsibility for carrying out our ministry—even during systems change—in a spirit of love.

For Reflection

- What stories of your denomination's founding can you recall? How could you place those before the congregation for contemporary reflection?

- What congregational traditions are unique to your context? How did they start? Why do they continue? What needs to retire?

- As you consider the local traditions of your congregation in light of Abram and Sarai's call in Genesis 12, in Luke 10, and in the book of Acts, where do you see points of convergence between your congregation and the biblical narrative? Where do you see divergence?

- How would you begin a process of reflection within your congregation to help your church be guided by the Spirit during systems change?

———

SEVEN

Fulfilling the Law of Christ

Bear one another's burdens, and in this way you will fulfill the law of Christ.

—GALATIANS 6:2

The man, whom I shall call Richard, looked at me in astonishment and nodded his head, agreeing to let me anoint him with oil. Richard was the person who at every turn had resisted my efforts at leading change. He had spoken disparagingly of me to others, had organized resistance, disrespected me publicly, and in other ways made my life hard.[1] He did all of this in the name of preserving tradition. While he didn't formally have power over my job, he had substantial power in the church. I lost many nights of sleep because of Richard.

On this day I was in a meeting with a group of church leaders. As we prepared to close with prayer, Richard mentioned his upcoming employment review with his boss, about which he had considerable anxiety. The group murmured sympathetically. Unexpectedly, I felt a small softening of my own heart toward his fear. After all, his job could be on the line. Before I could talk myself out of it and even while a voice inside my head shouted all the ways Richard made my life hard and all the reasons it was time he suffered and why this would be poetic justice and maybe even God wanted him to suffer, I blurted out, "Would you like us to anoint you with oil and pray?" Those words surely came from God and not from my offended self.

"Yes," he said, a bit dazed. "That would be so helpful." So I took out the oil, we anointed him and prayed. This occurred after he had uttered his usual complaints and grim forecasts.

While I can't say that *Richard's* attitude changed after this anointing, *I* experienced a change of my heart. The compassion that the Holy Spirit gave me to pray for him remained with me. As a result, Richard no longer had the power to dominate my thoughts or emotions with his negative energy. A small space opened in me into which God placed a tiny seed of kindness toward Richard.

I cannot take credit for what happened in that experience. It was truly a gift of God. While I frequently pray for the Holy Spirit to fill me anew and I sincerely desire to be a person who loves others, I am still subject to having my feelings hurt, obsessing about the offenses of others, and focusing on obstacles. My experience with Richard taught me a crucial lesson about how God works.

For much of history we in the Western church have tended to describe God in terms of magisterial power: God the mighty King, God the Master, the "three-omni" God, and such.[2] A trip to any art museum in the Western world displays the prevalence of these images of God that have shaped our collective imagination. We may direct our prayers to God the omnipotent mighty king believing that when we do God's will, this mighty God will make others do

> **God the Trinity is more like three spry, tireless, fearless, and relentless grandmothers plotting the salvation of the world.**

what we want or need. When that strong-arm approach fails, a crisis of faith can arise. We may even feel betrayed.

I am increasingly coming to understand God's personality and method as less like Zeus, smiting people who don't comply, or being two men and a bird orchestrating events to go in their direction. God the Trinity is more like three spry, tireless, fearless and relentless grandmothers plotting the salvation of the world. The "omni" qualities of God work through love and collaboration, relentless divine fidelity, creativity, and presence. Instead of working by brute force, they work with us—to the degree that we are open. Conversely, we can thwart their efforts when we close ourselves off. In doing so we cause God to suffer more than we can know.

The phrase "the fullness of time" (*kairos*) may refer less to pages turning on a divine calendar until the appointed hour and more to the fruition of events and circumstances because of our openness to God. Our collaboration with divine intent gets the job done.

Openness to God happens whenever we experience wonder, curiosity, compassion, love, or beauty. It happens when we suffer. Any life experience that causes us to long for meaning, for transcendence, for whatever is of God's character opens us to God. This is true whether we are religious or nonreligious, individuals or communities. God chooses to work collaboratively and cocreatively with us wherever we are open. And as Jesus teaches in the parable of the mustard seed (see Matthew 13:31-32), even a tiny degree of faith is enough for God to initiate a process that will in time become an astounding work of loving transformation. In this way, God makes all things new.

> **When we have even a tiny possibility of compassion for our opponents, God can change our hearts and the dynamics in a congregation.**

Wesleyan theology refers to "prevenient grace," God's love, initiative, and compassion that reaches out to us before we reach out to God. God demonstrating prevenient grace is like the mother who cooks dinner, sets the table, then goes to the door and calls us to come and eat. When she doesn't see us, she goes out and looks for us and brings us to the table. She has gone ahead of us, getting things ready. She does this because she loves us.

We witness this aspect of God in the stories of the Gospels where Jesus goes out bearing the news of God's love as he preaches, teaches, and heals people. Jesus often goes to them before they ask for him or know him. Going is his idea. Jesus loves across every wall that sin has built. Jesus looks for openings of faith, never forcing anyone to repent or to do God's will. Is the rich man open? Not yet, so Jesus lets him go on his way. This does not mean Jesus never gives the man another chance. It means he does not force the man to change at that time. (For the full story, read Mark 10:17-27.) The same practice is at work when Jesus meets the Samaritan woman at the well in John 4. He introduces her to living water, and she becomes the first evangelist in the Gospels because he seeks and finds openness in her. Her spiritual wondering about the right place and the right way to worship God is all Jesus needs to launch change. He needs her wonder.

Compassion and Change of Heart

As I found in my surprising encounter with Richard, when we have even a tiny possibility of compassion for our opponents, God can change our hearts and the dynamics in a congregation. The key to change comes in cultivating openness to God, first in ourselves and then in our community.

Paul brings his epistle to the Galatians to a close with a set of short instructions. All of us should work for the common good. If any of us in our congregation find ourselves in error, having made a poor choice, may the correction be gentle. We may be the next to stumble, and the thought of responding harshly to other Christians' failures is always a temptation. "If anyone is detected in a transgression, you who have received the Spirit should restore such a one in a spirit of gentleness" (Gal. 6:1). Responding in gentleness creates a powerful opening through which God can work much good.

The law of Christ, writes Paul, is to bear one another's burdens. The way forward in a congregation that suffers from systems change anxiety comes in creating openings for God by bearing one another's burdens. This includes learning to reconnect with one another at a deeper level, forming genuine friendships, spending time together, praying and helping one another with life.

The strongest quality a congregation can exhibit in its community is to love well—within and beyond the walls of the church.

Rev. Beth Crissman, an ordained elder in The United Methodist Church and a mental health nurse, is a behavioral change expert. She, along with her husband, Rev. Kelly Crissman, has worked with hundreds of declining congregations across the United States.[3] The foundational premise of their ministry, Plowpoint, is that when congregations begin to decline, people within the congregation inevitably are behaving badly. They have forgotten how to bear one another's burdens and failed to love well. They have become the congregation that Paul warns against when he says, "If, however, you bite and devour one another, take care that you are not consumed by one another" (Gal. 5:15). Plowpoint leads congregations through a process to change behavior so that once again they can "bear one another's burdens, and in this way . . . fulfill the law of Christ" (Gal. 6:2).

The strongest quality a congregation can exhibit in its community is to love well—within and beyond the walls of the church. Our neighbors do not need more preaching, more warnings about hell, or more gimmicks to get them to church on Sunday morning. They need our presence and our love. They need our humility. They need us to be church for them by bearing their burdens; in that way we will indeed fulfill the law of Christ.

For Reflection

- At the beginning of this chapter I talked about Richard and his resistance to necessary change. What did you think and feel as you read this story?

- How does a congregation continue to move forward lovingly even when the "Richards" do not change their negative tones?

- In what ways can your congregation support the work of your leaders, both clergy and laity, as you embrace systems change?

- As you consider your own context, what practices within your congregation give expression to loving well?

- In what ways do you dream of your congregation becoming better at "bearing one another's burdens, and in this way . . . fulfill the law of Christ"? What first steps will help you live into that dream?

———

A Letter to the Church

May the grace of our Lord Jesus Christ be with your spirit, brothers and sisters. Amen.
—GALATIANS 6:18

Dear church, God's one holy, catholic, and apostolic church:

First, I want to thank you for all that you have done for me and countless others. I don't know what would have happened to me if you had not come along and welcomed me into your fold. You have shaped my whole life since then, Mother Church. My vocation, which you pointed out to me before I recognized it in myself, is to help you keep living into yours.

So let's get on with our work. You know the parable of the wineskins. For goodness' sake, you taught that parable to me! We are in a time of wineskin change. Let's celebrate that instead of wringing our hands. Let's thank God for the old wineskin and the grace it carried to us. And let's celebrate the new wineskin with its expansive fermentation. Let's do both. We don't have to choose.

So what if we are losing our privileged place in society? We never did our best work there anyway. We're always our best on the bottom or the edge. This is a great time to remember the saints and mystics who founded our traditions, the ones who did their work from the margins.

Because—and I say this with more love than I can name—we can't afford to keep squabbling about things like buildings, budgets, pews, stoles, handbells, praise bands, and carpet. We can't keep acting like ministry is the work of the people with master's degrees and being served is the role for everyone else. We must stop that at once. God needs all hands on deck. We cannot continue operating as if we are a private club with members, dues, and privileges. Why? Because Jesus never acts like that. Our neighbors need us. God needs us. We need us too.

I know it's hard to play and be creative when we feel fearful. Anxiety takes the spring out of our step. It can trigger a vast array of responses: hunker down, raise fists, run and hide. But we don't have to be afraid. That is the wonderful news. God's love casts out fear. God is with us. With *us*! God orchestrates systems change. Change happens all the time so that every generation, every community, every person can experience God in their world, their context, their time. And what about the wave of change that is upon the church, the new ministries that look different from the church we grew up with? These are from God not the devil.

Beloved church, can we agree to let God have our anxiety? God knows how hard it is for us to let go. We simply have to be willing to be made willing. Just a tiny degree of openness allows God to work with us—like dandelion seeds. They blow on the wind, fall into every crack in the asphalt—and before you know it a parking lot is in full bloom. Church, do you realize we are on the cusp of a new Great Awakening? And it looks like a spiritual dandelion explosion as far as the eye can see. God's new thing is networked, exponential, Spirit-breathed, decentralized, a vast planting of small communities of faith that birth small communities of faith that continue to multiply. It is very much the work of laypeople, and it is emerging as a natural progression out of the church that used to be.

Can we give up our obsession with being big and making money? Can we learn from Jesus' journey in the wilderness immediately following his baptism? One reason we have resisted the new work that God is doing, beloved church, is that we buy into the foolishness that bigger is always better, that we have to make a big splash to get everyone's attention. We listen to the voice that tells us not to undertake a work unless we are assured it will make money and get big. This is not the voice of God because it does not agree with the way Jesus lived. Rather, it is the voice of Satan in the wilderness, tempting us to the world's notions of success in the same way he tempted Jesus. (Read Matthew 4:1-11.)

This is the day of small beginnings, and it is the day to rejoice over small beginnings. To use Jesus' metaphor of the mustard seed, the outcome of small beginnings will be more than we can imagine. Sustainability? Ask the mustard seed how it sustains itself. Our answer lies therein.

It is time for us to ask a better set of questions about being a vital church. Rather than counting Sunday morning worship numbers and the amount of money in the offering plate, let's raise questions about how people are living through the week. How is the church contributing to the flourishing of its neighborhood? In what ways are people in the church being equipped to bear the gospel into their own neighborhoods and workplaces? In what ways is the church living up to its baptismal vows to resist evil and injustice in whatever forms they present themselves? Questions like this help us live as bread and wine, given to the world.

I know if we will say yes to God, we can rely on God's already having said yes to us. So let's go together, all of us, in the direction that God leads. When that happens, the world will know that Jesus spoke the truth, that God's love is for everyone. People will encounter the real tradition, the tradition behind the tradition, because they will experience it in us.

NOTES

Introduction

1. The Celts used the metaphor of Wild Goose to name the Holy Spirit. For a well-researched, inspiring, and readable account of Celtic Christianity see Timothy Joyce, *Celtic Christianity: A Sacred Tradition, a Vision of Hope* (Maryknoll, NY: Orbis, 1998).

2. Elaine A. Heath, *The Mystic Way of Evangelism: A Contemplative Vision for Christian Outreach* (Grand Rapids, MI: Baker Academic, 2008).

3. The Prayer Foundation, "Dietrich Bonhoeffer on Prayer," http://prayerfoundation.org/dietrich_bonhoeffer_on_monasticism. htm; Thomas Merton, "The Christian in the Diaspora" in *Seeds of Destruction* (New York: Farrar, Straus and Giroux, 1964), 213; Karl Rahner, *Free Speech in the Church* (New York: Sheed and Ward, 1959), 86; Henri J. M. Nouwen, *In the Name of Jesus: Reflections on Christian Leadership* (New York: Crossroad, 1989, 2002), 42–47.

4. The story of the birth and ongoing development of the Missional Wisdom Foundation is described in Elaine A. Heath and Larry Duggins, *Missional.Monastic.Mainline: A Guide to Starting Missional Micro-Communities in Historic Mainline Traditions* (Eugene, OR: Cascade, 2014). This book is a sequel to Elaine A. Heath and Scott T. Kisker, *Longing for Spring: A New Vision for Wesleyan Community* (Eugene, OR: Cascade, 2010).

5. www.missionalwisdom.com.

6. In saying that God wasn't particularly Jewish I am not dismissing Judaism or disrespecting the Hebrew Bible. Rather I am referring to God being the Creator of the cosmos and Christ being savior of Jews and Gentiles alike. Jesus was indeed a thorough-going Jew. Through Jesus and Judaism, God revealed the divine intent to save the world. But the gospel according to Jesus is not confined to Judaism. Jesus himself said to a despised outsider, a Samaritan woman, that a time was coming when those who worship God will do so not by worshiping in Jerusalem *or* the holy place for Samaritans but in Spirit and in truth (John 4:5-42). The Gospel of John is especially oriented toward the cosmic authority and saving intent of Christ for the whole world.

7. Liminal space refers to a season in which our certitudes about God and the world are thrown up in the air. The *limen* (a Latin word) whence the English *liminal* comes, is the threshold between one room and another. Liminal space represents a crossing over into a much larger vision of who God is and what God is doing in the world. It can feel upsetting and disorienting. No alternative way exists; we have to go through it!

8. Jesus uses the phrase "the least of these" in Matthew 25:31-46 to describe those who are weak, vulnerable, imprisoned, hungry, or naked. All who find themselves at the mercy of others because of social dislocation, persecution, or economic oppression fall within the category of "the least of these."

One Loving the Tradition behind the Tradition

1. Jesus' authority is also expressed through his life and stories found in the four Gospels, although at the time Paul wrote his epistle to the Galatians, the Gospels were not yet written. Many scholars believe Mark, the first Gospel, was written by 65–70 CE. The other

Gospels came later. Galatians is believed to have been written around 49 CE, before or just after the first Jerusalem Council.

2. A Christian mystic is someone who has been transformed by the direct experience of God in Christ so that he or she feels compelled to share the love of God with the world.

3. For a good start into a deeper study of the life and work of the apostle Paul, see Gerald F. Hawthorne, Ralph P. Martin, and Daniel G. Reid, eds., *Dictionary of Paul and His Letters* (Downers Grove, IL: InterVarsity Press, 1993). This resource contains more than two hundred articles from a theologically diverse array of scholars.

4. Acts calls him by his Hebrew name, Saul, until he undergoes conversion to Christ. After that he is usually called Paul. As a Roman citizen he would have had three names—his Roman name (Paulus); his Hebrew name (Saul); and his family name, which is unknown.

5. For an accessible scholarly article about Paul's wilderness experiences see N. T. Wright, "Paul, Arabia, and Elijah (Galatians 1:17)," *Journal of Biblical Literature*, vol. 115:683–92; reprinted on N. T. Wright Page, ntwrightpage.com/Wright_Paul_Arabia_Elijah.pdf. Scholars disagree on how to interpret the different versions of Paul's story that are found in Acts and Galatians. For a discussion of these differences see C. W. Hansen, "Letter to the Galatians," *Dictionary of Paul and His Letters*, eds. Gerald F. Hawthorne, Ralph P. Martin, and Daniel G. Reid (Downers Grove, IL: InterVarsity Press, 1993), 332–33.

6. See "Paul, Arabia, and Elijah (Galatians 1:17)" in *Journal of Biblical Literature*. N. T. Wright provides valuable insight on the parallels between Paul and Elijah in Paul's autobiographical narratives. Paul deliberately reinforces his own call as a prophet in the great tradition of Hebrew prophets.

7. The word *apostle* means "sent out." Many people today use the word *missional* based on the Latin word *missio*, which means "sent out." Whether we use the word *apostolic* or *missional* the truth remains that the triune God is out here, engaged in the world, and sending out people like Paul to bear the healing, reconciling, forgiving, making-all-things-new love of God into the world. God is an apostolic, missional God.

Two   Opening Ourselves to God

1. Jahnabi Barooah, "Study Shows How Prayer, Meditation Affect Brain Activity," *Huffington Post*, 10/18/2012, huffingtonpost. com/2012/10/18/how-does-prayer-meditation-affect-brain-activity_n_1974621.html.

2. Names and other identifying details have been changed to protect the privacy of persons in the story. Portions of this chapter were first published in an essay, Elaine A. Heath, "Snake Handling and Speaking in Tongues: Mysticism and Mission in the Methodist Tradition," *Radical Grace*, Fall 2009. Used with permission.

Three   Authority, Discernment, Call

1. Pilgrimage is an ancient spiritual practice that involves leaving behind the familiar, traveling as lightly as possible, and keeping an open heart in order to encounter God. Geographic pilgrimages usually involve travel to a sacred location such as Jerusalem, Taizé, Iona, and so on. Pilgrimage is both an external and internal journey of transformation. Often what is most transformative is not planned religious experiences at sacred sites but obstacles or unexpected challenges that surface along the way.

2. Wendy J. Miller, *Jesus Our Spiritual Director: A Pilgrimage through the Gospels* (Nashville, TN: Upper Room Books, 2004).

Four When Systems Change

1. This volume does not explore the passages in Paul's writing that condemn the LGBTQ community, especially Romans 1:26-27. For a substantial and responsible study of this topic, I recommend Mark Achtemeier, *The Bible's Yes to Same Sex Marriage: An Evangelical's Change of Heart* (Louisville, KY: Westminster/John Knox, 2014).

2. Richard Rohr, *Eager to Love: The Alternative Way of Francis of Assisi* (Cincinnati, OH: Franciscan Media, 2014), 33.

3. freshexpressions.org.uk and freshexpressionsus.org.

4. missionalwisdom.com.

5. Jonathan Wilson-Hartgrove is a primary leader and writer for the New Monastic Movement. His book, *New Monasticism: What It Has to Say to Today's Church* (Grand Rapids, MI: Brazos, 2008), makes a significant contribution that locates the new monastic movement in the long tradition of monastic renewal movements in the church. jonathanwilsonhartgrove.com. For a Methodist perspective on new monasticism and new forms of church see Elaine A. Heath and Scott T. Kisker, *Longing for Spring: A New Vision for Wesleyan Community* (Eugene, OR: Cascade, 2010), and Elaine A. Heath and Larry Duggins, *Missional.Monastic.Mainline: A Guide to Starting Missional Micro-Communities in Historically Mainline Traditions* (Eugene, OR: Cascade, 2014).

6. Helpful resources, both books and video, for understanding how systems change can be found in the work of Margaret Wheatley and Deborah Frieze, available on their website Walk Out Walk On, walkoutwalkon.net.

7. Richard Twiss, *Rescuing the Gospel from the Cowboys: A Native American Expression of the Jesus Way* (Downers Grove, IL: InterVarsity Press, 2015). Also see naiits.com, the website for North American

Institute of Indigenous Theological Studies, a new program in theological education that is shaped by First People cultures and led by
First People theologians and practitioners.

8. Phyllis Tickle has written insightfully about the phenomenon of culture shift that occurs every five hundred years and that
we are now experiencing, in her book *The Great Emergence: How
Christianity Is Changing and Why* (Grand Rapids, MI: Baker, 2008).
She further explores emergence in *Emergence Christianity: What It
Is, Where It Is Going, and Why It Matters* (Grand Rapids, MI: Baker,
2012).

Five   Responding to Anxiety in the System

1. One helpful book that teaches the prayer of examen in a way
that everyone can understand is Dennis Linn, Sheila Fabricant Linn,
and Matthew Linn, *Sleeping with Bread: Holding What Gives You Life*
(New York: Paulist Press, 1995). To introduce the congregation to
several forms of contemplative prayer I recommend the accessible
volume by David Keller, *Come and See: The Transformation of Personal Prayer* (New York: Morehouse, 2009).

2. Another book of mine that points congregations and leaders into a contemplative stance is *The Mystic Way of Evangelism: A
Contemplative Vision for Christian Outreach*. Most of the book is very
accessible to a lay audience. *The Mystic Way* focuses on learning from
the lives and teachings of some of the great Christian mystics, who
can help us reclaim our God-given vocation as the church.

Six   Guided by the Spirit

1. Edwin H. Friedman, *The Failure of Nerve: Leadership in the
Age of the Quick Fix* (New York: Seabury, 1999, 2007).

Seven Fulfilling the Law of Christ

1. I have changed the name and other identifying details of this event to protect the privacy of all persons involved.

2. Omniscient (all-knowing), omnipresent (present every-where), and omnipotent (all-powerful).

3. Plowpoint's website: plowpoint.org.

ABOUT THE AUTHOR

ELAINE A. HEATH is the dean of Duke Divinity School in Durham, North Carolina. An ordained elder in The United Methodist Church, she has served as a pastor in local churches as well as in academia. Elaine is the cofounder of the Missional Wisdom Foundation (www.missionalwisdom.com), a nonprofit that administers a national network of regional hubs of missional learning communities including new monastic houses, social enterprise, missionally repurposed church spaces, and training programs in missional theology, spiritual formation, and leadership development for a missional church.

Other Publications by Elaine A. Heath

The Mystic Way of Evangelism: A Contemplative Vision for Christian Outreach (Grand Rapids, MI: Baker Academic, 2008).

Naked Faith: The Mystical Theology of Phoebe Palmer (Eugene, OR: Wipf and Stock, Princeton Theological Monograph Series, 2009).

Longing for Spring: A New Vision for Wesleyan Community with Scott T. Kisker (Eugene, OR: Cascade, 2010).

We Were the Least of These: Reading the Bible with Survivors of Sexual Abuse (Grand Rapids, MI: Brazos, 2011).

The Gospel According to Twilight: Women, Sex and God (Louisville, KY: Westminster/John Knox, 2011).

Missional.Monastic.Mainline: A Guide to Starting Missional Communities in Historically Mainline Traditions, coauthored with Larry Duggins (Eugene, OR: Cascade, 2014).

for those who hunger for deep spiritual experience . . .

The Academy for Spiritual Formation® offers a place for spiritually hungry pilgrims, both clergy and lay, to find rest and renewal. A ministry of The Upper Room®, the Academy offers Two-Year or Five-Day experiences. During the Two-Year Academy, pilgrims gather at a retreat center for five days every three months over the course of two years (a total of 40 days) to worship, study, pray, fellowship, and learn. The Five-Day Academy, a modified version of the Two-Year experience, invites pilgrims to gather for five days of spiritual learning and worship.

Trained faculty in the subjects of Christian Spirituality, Spiritual Leadership, and Contemplative Prayer lead each session of The Academy. Author and theologian Elaine A. Heath has served as faculty for The Academy for over fifteen years.

The Academy's commitment to an authentic spirituality promotes balance, inner and outer peace, holy living and just living—God's shalom. Theologically, the focus is Trinitarian, celebrating the Creator's blessing, delighting in the companionship of Christ, and witnessing to the power of the Holy Spirit to transform lives, churches, and the world.

Do you hunger to learn and grow in Christian covenant community? The Academy is for you. Learn more here:

academy.upperroom.org

CPSIA information can be obtained
at www.ICGtesting.com
Printed in the USA
FSOW02n1929040517
33904FS

9 780835 815833